# DEEPENING LIFE TOGETHER

# JOHN

*LIFE TOGETHER*

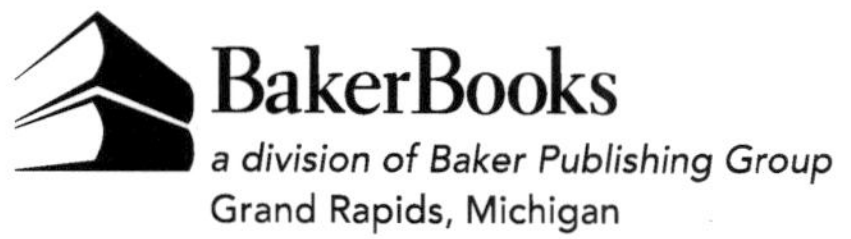

Published by Lamplighter Media
6755 Mira Mesa Blvd. #123-272
San Diego, CA 92121
www.GroupSpice.com

Printed in the United States of America



Library of Congress Cataloging-in-Publication Data
John / [editors, Mark L. Strauss, Teresa Haymaker].
p. cm. — (Deepening life together)
Includes bibliographical references.
ISBN 978-1-941326-20-6 (pbk.)
1. Bible. N.T. John—Textbooks. 2. Bible. N.T. John—Study and teaching. I. Strauss, Mark L. II. Haymaker, Teresa.
BS2616.J64 2009
226.5′0071—dc22 2009014247

# CONTENTS

# ACKNOWLEDGMENTS

The *Deepening Life Together: John* Small Group Video Bible Study has come together through the efforts of many at Baker Publishing Group, Lifetogether Publishing, and Lamplighter Media for which we express our heartfelt thanks.

| | |
|---|---|
| Executive Producer | John Nill |
| Producer and Director | Sue Doc Ross |
| Editors | Mark L. Strauss (Scholar), Teresa Haymaker |
| Curriculum Development | Brett Eastman, Sue Doc Ross, Jennifer Tiszai, Stephanie French, Teresa Haymaker, Mark L. Strauss, Karen Lee-Thorp |
| Video Production | Chris Balish, Rodney Bissell, Nick Calabrese, Sebastian Hoppe Fuentes, Josh Greene, Patrick Griffin, Teresa Haymaker, Oziel Jabin Ibarra, Natali Ibarra, Janae Janik, Keith Sorrell, Lance Tracy |
| Teachers and Scholars | Lynn Cohick, Alan Hultberg, Joanne Jung, Dennis Keating, Craig Keener, Mark Strauss, Erik Thoennes |
| Baker Publishing Group | Jack Kuhatschek |

Special thanks to DeLisa Ivy, Bethel Seminary, Talbot School of Theology, Wheaton College



Interior icons by Tom Clark

# READ ME FIRST

Most people want to live a healthy, balanced spiritual life, but few achieve this by themselves. And most small groups struggle to balance all of God's purposes in their meetings. Groups tend to overemphasize one of the five purposes, perhaps fellowship or discipleship. Rarely is there a healthy balance that includes evangelism, ministry, and worship. That's why we've included all of these elements in this study so you can live a healthy, balanced spiritual life over time.

A typical group session will include the following:

**Memory Verses**

For each session we have provided a memory verse that emphasizes an important truth from the session. This is an optional exercise, but we believe that memorizing Scripture can be a vital part of filling our minds with God's Word. We encourage you to give this important habit a try.

CONNECTING *with God's Family (Fellowship)*

The foundation for spiritual growth is an intimate connection with God and his family. A few people who really know you and who earn your trust provide a place to experience the life Jesus invites you to live. This section of each session typically offers you two activities. You can get to know your whole group by using the icebreaker question, and/or you can check in with one or two group members—your spiritual partner(s)—for a deeper connection and encouragement in your spiritual journey.

DVD TEACHING SEGMENT. A *Deepening Life Together: John* Video Teaching DVD companion to this study guide is available. For each study session, the DVD contains a lesson taught by Jim Garlow. If you are using the DVD, you will view the teaching segment after your *Connecting* discussion and before your group discussion time (the *Growing* section). At the end of each session in this study guide, you will find space for your notes on the teaching segment.

## GROWING *to Be Like Christ (Discipleship)*

Here is where you come face-to-face with Scripture. In core passages you'll explore what the Bible teaches about the topic of the study. The focus won't be on accumulating information but on how we should live in light of the Word of God. We want to help you apply the Scriptures practically, creatively, and from your heart as well as your head. At the end of the day, allowing the timeless truths from God's Word to transform our lives in Christ is our greatest aim.

## DEVELOPING *Your Gifts to Serve Others (Ministry)*

Jesus trained his disciples to discover and develop their gifts to serve others. And God has designed each of us uniquely to serve him in a way no other person can. This section will help you discover and use your God-given design. It will also encourage your group to discover your unique design as a community. In this study, you'll put into practice what you've learned in the Bible study by taking a step to serve others. These simple steps will take your group on a faith journey that could change your lives forever.

## SHARING *Your Life Mission Every Day (Evangelism)*

Many people skip over this aspect of the Christian life because it's scary, relationally awkward, or simply too much work for their busy schedules. But Jesus wanted all of his disciples to help outsiders connect with him, to know him personally. This doesn't mean preaching on street corners. It could mean welcoming a few newcomers into your group, hosting a short-term group in your home, or walking through this study with a friend. In this study, you'll have an opportunity to go beyond Bible study to biblical living.

## SURRENDERING *Your Life for God's Pleasure (Worship)*

God is most pleased by a heart that is fully his. Each group session will give you a chance to surrender your heart to God in prayer and worship. You may read a psalm together, share a page in your journal, or sing a song to close your meeting. If you have never prayed aloud in a group before, no one will pressure you. Instead, you'll experience the support of others who are praying for you.

### Study Notes

This section provides background notes on the Bible passage(s) you examine in the *Growing* section. You may want to refer to these notes during your group meeting or as a reference for those doing additional study.

### For Deeper Study (Optional)

If you want to dig deeper into more Bible passages about the topic at hand, we've provided additional passages and questions. Your group may choose to do study homework ahead of each meeting in order to cover more biblical material. Or you as an individual may choose to study the *For Deeper Study* on your own. If you prefer not to do study homework, the *Growing* section will provide you with plenty to discuss within the group. These options allow individuals or the whole group to go deeper in their study, while still accommodating those who can't do homework or are new to your group.

You can record your discoveries in your journal. We encourage you to read some of your insights to a friend (spiritual partner) for accountability and support. Spiritual partners may check in each week over the phone, through e-mail, or at the beginning of the group meeting.

**Reflections**

On the *Reflections* pages we provide Scriptures to read and reflect on between group meetings. We suggest you use this section to seek God at home throughout the week. This time at home should begin and end with prayer. Don't get in a hurry; take enough time to hear God's direction.

**Subgroup for Discussion and Prayer**

If your group is large (more than seven people), we encourage you to separate into groups of two to four for discussion and prayer. This is to encourage greater participation and deeper discussion.

# INTRODUCTION

Welcome to the *Deepening Life Together* series Bible study on the book of *John*. As we experience the next eight weeks together, John will take us through his eyewitness account of Jesus's life, ministry, death, and resurrection. As we read, discuss, and reflect on the topic of each session, we will discover how God demonstrated Jesus's true identity as the Messiah, the one through whom eternal life is gained.

As John's gospel begins, Jesus is revealed as the Word and creator of the heavens and the earth. He is the self revelation of God, who became a human being to bring light and life to all who believe in him. John relates various testimonies about Jesus's identity as Messiah and king of Israel. Though Jesus comes into conflict with Israel's leaders, through powerful signs and wonders he continues to reveal he is God's anointed one. The final "sign" of John's Gospel, the raising of Lazarus from the dead, serves as a preview of Jesus's own resurrection and offers further proof of his identity—the true fulfillment of Israel, the one who supplies the bread of life from heaven, the Messiah, and the good shepherd over God's flock.

This journey of discovery will make known God's purposes for our lives. We will connect with our loving and faithful God and with other believers in small group community. We will become his hands and feet here on earth as he reveals our uniqueness and his willingness to use us. We will experience the closeness that he desires with us as we prayerfully respond to the principles we learn in this study and learn to place him first in our lives.

We at Baker Books and Lifetogether Publishing look forward to hearing the stories of how God changes you from the inside out during this small group experience. We pray God blesses you with all he has planned for you through this journey together.

> For the LORD is good and his love endures forever;
> his faithfulness continues through all generations.
>
> Psalm 100:5 (NIV)

SESSION ONE

# THE PROLOGUE OF JOHN

**Memory Verse: In the beginning was the Word, and the Word was with God, and the Word was God (John 1:1 NIV).**

Words, when used effectively, are powerful. They can demolish aspirations; they can provoke war; and they can destroy relationships. On the other hand, words can inspire lives and transform ideas; they can propagate peace between nations; they can take us on journeys to places we've never been; they can provide hope for the oppressed.

God has demonstrated the power of his words throughout Scripture. He used the spoken word to create the universe and its inhabitants, to judge Satan after the fall, to offer the promise of reconciliation, and as we'll see in the beginning of John, God uses *the Word* to draw us into a relationship with himself.

## Connecting

Prayer is a powerful way to connect as a group. Open your group with prayer and invite the Holy Spirit to lead you as you begin to learn about the life of Jesus Christ through the book of John.

Deeper relationships happen when we take the time to keep in touch with one another between sessions. As you begin, pass around a copy of the *Small Group Roster*, a sheet of paper, or one of you pass your study guide, opened to the *Small Group Roster*. When the roster gets to you, write down your contact information, including the best time and method for contacting you. Then, someone volunteer to make copies or type up a list with everyone's information and e-mail it to the group this week.

1. Begin this first session by introducing yourselves. Include your name and what you do for fun. You may also include whether or not you are married and how long you have been married, how many children you have, and their ages. Also share what brought you to this small group study of John and what you expect to learn during the next eight weeks.

2. Whether your group is new or ongoing, it's always important to reflect on and review your values together. In the *Appendix* is a *Small Group Agreement* with the values most useful in developing and sustaining healthy, balanced small groups. Choose two or three values that you haven't previously focused on, or have room to grow in, to emphasize during this study. Choose values that will take your group to the next stage of intimacy and spiritual health.

   If your group is new, you may want to focus on welcoming newcomers or on sharing group ownership. Any group will quickly move from being *the leader's group* to *our group* when everyone understands the goals of the group and shares a small role in accomplishing them. See the *Team Roles* in the *Appendix* for help on how to do this well.

3. Are you a letter or Christmas card writer? In one or two sentences, why or why not?

## Growing

The Gospel of John begins with a narrative explanation of the nature and person of Christ and the meaning of faith in him. John's driving purpose in writing this Gospel is to establish Jesus as the Son of God and Messiah.

To get started, please read John 1:1–18 aloud.

4. John begins his Gospel with the phrase, "In the beginning was the Word." What does John 1:1–5 tell us about the Word? (See the *Study Notes* for more insight into the meanings of beginning and the Word.)

   What is significant about calling him "the Word"?

5. Compare John 1:1–2 with Genesis 1:1. What similarities do you see in these verses? What point do you think John is trying to make?

6. Now compare John 1:14 with what you read in John 1:1–2. Who do you understand the Word to be? Why?

   How does 1:3–5 define the role of the Word in creation and in our lives?

7. In John 1:6–8 we learn that God sent John the Baptist. What was John sent to do?

   How is our role in the world similar to John the Baptist's?

8. To whom did Jesus come first? What was the result (John 1:10–11)?

9. How are the people described in 1:12–13 different from the ones in 1:10–11?

   What does it mean to be "born of God"?

10. How did Jesus reveal his glory according to John 1:14?

What does this verse show us about God's character?

11. Although no one has ever seen God the Father, God the Son (Jesus) has revealed him through what he said and did. Why do you think it is important that Jesus came to us in human form? (See John 1:18, as well as Col. 1:15–20 and Heb. 1:3 for additional insight.)

12. According to John 1:17, the law was given through Moses. Turn to Deuteronomy 32:46–47 and read these verses aloud. How important was the law to the Israelite people according to these verses?

13. Grace and truth came through Jesus Christ (John 1:17b). How would you describe the difference between what Moses gave us and what Jesus gave us? See the *Study Notes* for definitions of grace and truth.

14. What is one thing about Jesus as described in John 1:1–18 that is important for you personally right now? Why does that truth about him matter to you?

John 1:1–18 is a literary masterpiece that summarizes the Gospel's main theme: Jesus the Word and Creator is the self-revelation of God who became a human being to bring light and life to all who believe in him.

## Developing

Jesus came to earth to fulfill a specific purpose. Each of us has been given a purpose by God to fulfill. But we can only discover that purpose by spending time in the Bible and in prayer.

15. Developing our ability to serve God according to the leading of the Holy Spirit requires that we make time to let God speak to us daily. Which of the following next steps toward this goal are you willing to take for the next few weeks?

- ☐ **Prayer.** Commit to connecting with God daily through personal prayer. It's important to separate yourself from the distractions in your life so you can really focus on communicating with God.
- ☐ **Reflection.** At the end of each session, you'll find *Reflections* Scriptures that specifically relate to the topic of our study each week. These are provided to give you an opportunity for reading a short Bible passage five days a week during the course of this study. Write down your insights on what you read each day in the space provided. On the sixth day, summarize what God has shown you throughout the week.
- ☐ **Meditation.** Psalm 119:11 says, "I have hidden your word in my heart that I might not sin against you" (NIV). Meditation is focused attention on the Word of God and is a great way to internalize God's Word more deeply. One way to do this is to write a portion of Scripture on a card and tape it somewhere where you're sure to see it often, such as your bathroom mirror, your car's dashboard, or the kitchen table. Think about it as you get dressed in the morning, when you sit at red lights, or while you're eating a meal. Reflect on what God is saying to you through his words. Consider using the passages provided in the *Reflections* pages in each session. As you meditate upon these Scriptures, you will notice them beginning to take up residence in your heart and mind.

## Sharing

Jesus lived and died so that humanity might come to know him and be reconciled to God through him. His final words before his ascension as recorded in Acts 1:8 were: "You will receive power when the Holy Spirit comes on you; and you will be my witnesses in Jerusalem, and in all Judea and Samaria, and to the ends of the earth . . ." (NIV). Through the Holy Spirit, we are empowered to be his witnesses to those around us.

16. Jesus wanted all of his disciples to help others connect with him, to know him personally. In the weeks to come, you'll be asked to identify and share with people in your circle of influence who need to know Jesus or need to connect with him through a small group community. With this in mind, as you go about your day-to-day activities this week, pay special attention to the people God has placed in your life. There may be co-workers, family or friends, or other parents at school or sporting events whom you see or talk to on a regular basis. When we meet next week, we'll talk about how we can begin sharing Jesus with those who don't yet know him as well as how to help connect believers to Christian community.

## Surrendering

Just as Jesus was fully surrendered to the Father when he came to earth to do his will, we find our purpose when we surrender ourselves fully to God.

17. Every believer should have a plan for spending time alone with God. Your time with God is personal and reflects who you are in relationship with our God. However you choose to spend your time with him, try to allow time for praise, prayer, and reading of Scripture. *Reflections* are provided at the end of each session for you to use as part of your daily time with him. These will offer reinforcement of the principles we are learning, and develop or strengthen your habit of time alone with God throughout the week.

18. Before you close your group in prayer, allow everyone to answer this question: "How can we pray for you this week?" Write prayer requests on your *Prayer and Praise Report* and commit to praying for each other throughout the week.

## Study Notes

***Word (Logos):*** *Logos* means "word, message, report" and sometimes even "deed." *Logos* is also used to refer to Jesus as God's revelation of himself. Jesus was the *Logos* eternally, but at a point in history he took on human flesh.

***Beginning:*** The same term is used in the Greek translation of Genesis 1:1 where it assumes a timeless eternity, highlighting the eternal preexistence of the Word (Jesus Christ). Jesus has universal rather than local significance and he speaks with ultimate authority.

***Grace:*** Underserved acceptance and love received from another, especially the characteristic attitude of God in providing salvation for sinners. The gospel speaks of God's gift of unmerited salvation in Jesus Christ.

***Truth:*** Something that is accurate, real. But truth is not only in statements. This term can be used to describe God himself, who is the ultimate standard of what is true and real.

## For Deeper Study (Optional)

Read through John 1; note the titles Jesus is given. How does John's inclusion of these titles further demonstrate his purpose in writing this Gospel account?

- The Word (v. 1)
- The Light (v. 5)
- The One and Only (v. 14)
- The Lamb of God (v. 29)
- The Son of God (v. 34)
- Rabbi (v. 38)
- Messiah (v. 40)

- The One Moses wrote about in the law (v. 45)
- The son of Joseph (v. 45)
- King of Israel (v. 49)
- Son of Man (v. 51)

## Reflections

Reading, reflecting, and meditating on the Word of God is essential to getting to know him deeply. As you read the verses each day, give prayerful consideration to what you learn about God, his Spirit, and his place in your life. Then record your thoughts, insights, or prayer in the *Reflect* section below the verses you read. On the sixth day, record a summary of what you learned over the entire week through this study.

***Day 1.*** The Son reflects God's own glory, and everything about him represents God exactly. He sustains the universe by the mighty power of his command. After he died to cleanse us from the stain of sin, he sat down in the place of honor at the right hand of the majestic God of heaven (Heb. 1:3 NLT).

REFLECT

______________________________________________

______________________________________________

______________________________________________

______________________________________________

***Day 2.*** Christ is the visible image of the invisible God. He existed before God made anything at all and is supreme over all creation. Christ is the one through whom God created everything in heaven and earth. He made the things we can see and the things we can't see—kings, kingdoms, rulers, and authorities. Everything has been created through him and for him. He existed before everything else began, and he holds all creation together (Col. 1:15–17 NLT).

REFLECT

*Day 3.* That which was from the beginning, which we have heard, which we have seen with our eyes, which we have looked at and our hands have touched—this we proclaim concerning the Word of life (1 John 1:1 NIV).

REFLECT

*Day 4.* He made himself nothing; he took the humble position of a slave and appeared in human form. And in human form he obediently humbled himself even further by dying a criminal's death on a cross (Phil. 2:7–8 NLT).

REFLECT

***Day* 5.** And I heard a loud voice from the throne saying, "Now the dwelling of God is with men, and he will live with them. They will be his people, and God himself will be with them and be their God (Rev. 21:3 NIV).

REFLECT

______________________________________________

______________________________________________

______________________________________________

______________________________________________

***Day* 6.** Use the following space to write any thoughts God has put in your heart and mind about the things we have looked at in this session and during your *Reflections* time this week.

SUMMARY

______________________________________________

______________________________________________

______________________________________________

______________________________________________

SESSION TWO

# FIRST SIGN FROM THE MESSIAH

**Memory Verse: John saw Jesus coming toward him and said, "Look, the Lamb of God, who takes away the sin of the world!" (John 1:29 NIV).**

Areas of the American Southwest often experience droughtlike and windy conditions and are known for wildfires. In extreme or dangerous situations, aerial firefighting methods are employed during which air tankers drop hundreds of gallons of water or fire retardant on the flames from above. Spotter aircraft circle the fire at a higher altitude to coordinate the efforts and lead planes fly ahead of larger air tankers to mark the trajectory for the drop. These spotters and lead planes alert the ground firefighters of the impending drop, allowing those on the ground to be prepared.

John the Baptist was Jesus's spotter, or lead plane. Spoken of by the prophet Isaiah in Isaiah 40:3, his was, "A voice of one calling: 'In the desert prepare the way for the LORD; make straight in the wilderness a highway for our God'" (NIV). John was sent in advance to preach of repentance for the forgiveness of sins so that his followers would be prepared for Jesus's eventual arrival.

## Connecting

Open your group with prayer and prepare your hearts to learn about the beginning of Jesus's ministry and how that allowed us to become members of his family.

1. If you have new people joining you for the first time, take a few minutes to briefly introduce yourselves.

2. Healthy small groups rotate leadership. We recommend that you rotate leaders on a regular basis. This practice helps to develop every member's ability to shepherd a few people within a safe environment. Even Jesus gave others the opportunity to serve alongside him (Mark 6:30–44).

   It's also a good idea to rotate host homes, with the host of each meeting providing the refreshments. Some groups like to let the host lead the meeting each week, while others like to allow one person to host while another person leads.

   The *Small Group Calendar* is a tool for planning who will lead and host each meeting. Take a few minutes to plan leaders and hosts for your remaining meetings. Don't pass up this opportunity! It will revolutionize your group.

   For information on leading your group, see the *Leader's Notes (Introduction)* in the *Appendix*. Also, if you are leading for the first time, see *Leading for the First Time (Leadership 101)* in the *Appendix*. Also refer to the *Frequently Asked Questions (FAQs)*.

3. Share what you do for a living and how you came to be in that job. Was it a choice or was it something you "fell into"?

## Growing

In this session we'll look at how John the Baptist's testimony served as a springboard for Jesus's earthly ministry. Jesus called his first disciples and performed his first miracle, symbolizing the coming age of salvation.

Begin by reading John 1:19–2:12 aloud.

4. When John the Baptist is called before the Jews, he denies he is the Christ (Messiah). Who does he say he is (John 1:23; Isa. 40:3)?

   Why do you think John quotes Isaiah 40:3 to identify himself to the Jews? What is his point?

5. John testifies that while he baptizes with water, Christ will baptize with the Holy Spirit. What does that mean?

   What does he mean by calling Jesus "the Lamb of God" (1:32–34)?

   Why is John's testimony about seeing the Spirit descend on Jesus important to launching Jesus's ministry?

6. Read John 1:37–42 aloud. What impression do you get of Jesus from the way he interacts with John's followers and their friends?

7. What do you learn about Jesus from the way he interacts with Nathanael (1:43–51)?

   What do you think is the meaning of Jesus's promise to Nathanael?

8. Jesus performs his first miracle, or sign, at a wedding in Cana, a village of Galilee (2:1–12). At his mother's request, Jesus prevents a huge social embarrassment to the wedding family by turning water into wine. How does this act reveal Jesus's "glory" (2:11)? (See the *Study Notes* on glory.)

9. Read Isaiah 25:6–8. Why is wine at a wedding banquet a fitting beginning to Jesus's ministry? (See the *Study Notes* for insight into the messianic banquet and age of salvation.)

10. Most people in our culture don't witness the kind of miracles the disciples witnessed that brought them to faith in Christ. How do you think God brings people to faith in Christ today?

    How have you seen Christ's "glory"?

The beginning of John's Gospel recounts various testimonies about Jesus's identity and the first miracle at Cana of Galilee. The latter symbolizes the new age of salvation that is about to be inaugurated through Jesus's life, death, and resurrection.

## Developing

Spiritual accountability happens when we invite someone into our lives for the purpose of encouraging us in our faith journeys and challenging us in specific areas where we need or desire growth. Hebrews 3:12–13 read: "See to it, brothers, that none of you has a sinful, unbelieving heart that turns away from the living God. But encourage one another daily, as long as it is called Today, so that none of you may be hardened by sin's deceitfulness" (NIV). Opening our lives to someone and making ourselves vulnerable to their loving admonition could perhaps be one of the most difficult things we do but could result in the deepest and most lasting spiritual growth we've known.

11. Scripture tells us in Ephesians 4:25 "SPEAK TRUTH EACH ONE of you WITH HIS NEIGHBOR, for we are members of one another" (NASB). With this in mind, take a moment to pair up with someone in your group to be your spiritual partner for the remaining weeks of this study (men partner with men and women with women). Once you have done this, turn to the *Personal Health Plan.*

    In the box that says, "WHO are you connecting with spiritually?" write your partner's name. In the box that says, "WHAT is your next step for growth?" write one step you would like to take for growth during this study. Tell your partner what step you chose. When you check in with your partner each week, the

"Partner's Progress" column on this chart will provide a place to record your partner's progress in the goal he or she chose.

12. Spending time getting to know each other outside of group meetings is helpful to building stronger relationships within your group. Discuss whether your group would like to have a potluck or other type of social to celebrate together what God is doing in your group. You could plan to share a meal prior to a small group meeting or plan to follow your completion of this study with a barbecue. Appoint one or two people who can follow up with everyone outside of group time to put a plan together.

## Sharing

Just as Simon and Nathanael were brought to Jesus by people they knew, we can play a powerful role in introducing people in our lives to Jesus.

13. Take a look at the *Circles of Life* diagram (next page) and write the names of two or three people in each circle whom you come in contact with on a regular basis who need to be connected in Christian community.

    The people who fill these circles are not there by accident. God has strategically placed each of them within your sphere of influence because he has equipped you to minister to them and share with them in ways no one else can. Consider the following ideas for reaching out to one or two of the people you listed and make a plan to follow through with them this week.

    - ☐ This is a wonderful time to welcome a few friends into your group. Which of the people you listed could you invite? It's possible that you may need to help your friend overcome obstacles to coming to a place where he or she can encounter Jesus. Does your friend need a ride to the group or help with child care?
    - ☐ Consider inviting a friend to attend a weekend church service with you and possibly plan to enjoy a meal together

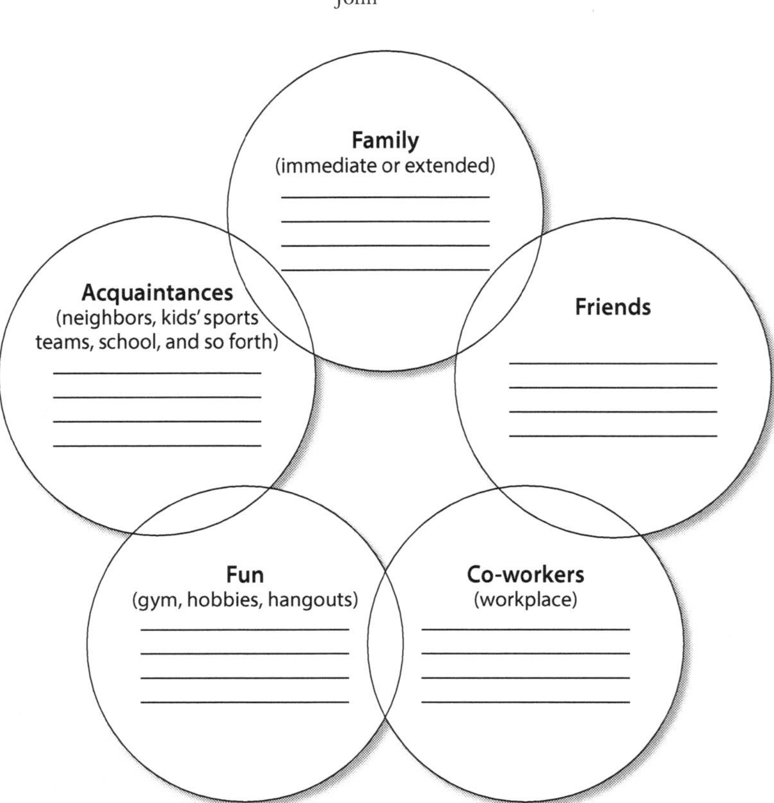


afterward. This can be a great opportunity to talk with someone about your faith in Jesus.

☐ Is there someone who is unable to attend your group but who still needs a connection? Would you be willing to have lunch or coffee with that person, catch up on life, and share something you've learned from this study? Jesus doesn't call all of us to lead small groups, but he does call every disciple to spiritually multiply his or her life over time.

## Surrendering

Jesus took regular time away from everyone and everything to be alone with his father and pray. Praying for one another is one way we grow closer to each other and to God.

14. Share your prayer requests in your group and then gather in smaller circles of three or four people to pray. Be sure to have everyone write down the personal requests of the members to use as a reminder to pray for your group throughout the week. Don't put pressure on anyone to pray aloud. When you pray for each person, you may find it meaningful to hold hands or place your hands on another person's shoulder. Jesus often touched people to communicate his care for them.

15. Take a few minutes to talk about what it would take to make time with God a priority every day or even five or six days a week. Don't put time demands on yourself at first; just make it a priority to draw near to God for a few minutes each day and gradually you will desire more. Use the *Reflections* at the end of each session as a starting point.

## Study Notes

***Name:*** A name (Simon, or Peter) often represented the nature or character of a person. Names demonstrated a broad range of meanings including personality, authority, and reputation. Changing a person's name expressed either exaltation to a new dignity or a reduction to dependency.

***Belief:*** A person's trusting commitment to God.

***Messianic Banquet:*** In both the Old and New Testaments, banquets are prominent in sealing friendships, in celebrating victories, and for other joyous occasions. Jesus's turning water to wine at the wedding in Cana symbolized the messianic banquet (Isa. 25:6–8), an Old Testament picture of God's end-time salvation and God's final victory over sin and death. The "marriage supper of the Lamb" of God in Revelation 19:9 is another picture of this great banquet. Jesus also told parables comparing God's kingdom to a banquet.

***Age of Salvation:*** The age of salvation is the time inaugurated by the ascension of Christ and the coming of the Holy Spirit. It is the time when those who come to Christ can be saved through faith in him. It will last until the return of Christ.

***Glory:*** The weighty importance and shining majesty that accompany God's presence.

## For Deeper Study (Optional)

1. Read John 1:39, 46. Philip mirrors Jesus's words "come and see." What does this say about the power of testimony, personal experience, and relationships in bringing people to Christ?

2. There is an interesting exchange between Jesus and his mother in John 2:3–5. Why do you think she came to him when the family ran out of wine? How do her attitude and her instructions to the servant represent submission?

3. In John 2:10 we see that people usually served cheaper wine later in the reception. But Jesus turned the water into the best wine. What conclusions can we draw from Jesus doing this?

## Reflections

Hopefully last week you made a commitment to read, reflect, and meditate on the Word of God each day. Following are selections of Scripture provided as a starting point to drawing near to God through time with him. Read the daily verses and then record your thoughts, insights, or prayers in the space provided. On the sixth day, record a summary of what you have learned over the entire week through this study or use this space to write down how God has challenged you personally.

*Day 1.* As soon as Jesus was baptized, he went up out of the water. At that moment heaven was opened, and he saw the Spirit of God descending like a dove and lighting on him. And a voice from heaven said, "This is my Son, whom I love; with him I am well pleased" (Matt. 3:16–17 NIV).

REFLECT

____________________

____________________

____________________

____________________

*Day 2.* Now the passage of Scripture which he was reading was this: "HE WAS LED AS A SHEEP TO SLAUGHTER; AND AS A LAMB BEFORE ITS SHEARER IS SILENT, SO HE DOES NOT OPEN HIS MOUTH" (Acts 8:32 NASB).

REFLECT

____________________

____________________

____________________

____________________

*Day 3.* One day as Jesus was walking along the shore beside the Sea of Galilee, he saw two brothers—Simon, also called Peter, and Andrew—fishing with a net, for they were commercial fishermen. Jesus called out to them, "Come, be my disciples, and I will show you how to fish for people!" (Matt. 4:18–19 NLT).

REFLECT

____________________

____________________

____________________

____________________

*Day 4*. But Jesus said, "Foxes have dens to live in, and birds have nests, but I, the Son of Man, have no home of my own, not even a place to lay my head" (Matt. 8:20 NLT).

REFLECT

______________________________________________

______________________________________________

______________________________________________

______________________________________________

*Day 5*. As my vision continued that night, I saw someone who looked like a man coming with the clouds of heaven. He approached the Ancient One and was led into his presence. He was given authority, honor, and royal power over all the nations of the world, so that people of every race and nation and language would obey him. His rule is eternal—it will never end. His kingdom will never be destroyed (Dan. 7:13–14 NLT).

REFLECT

______________________________________________

______________________________________________

______________________________________________

______________________________________________

*Day 6*. Use this space to record insights, thoughts, or prayers that God has given you during *Session Two* and your *Reflections* time.

SUMMARY

______________________________________________

______________________________________________

______________________________________________

______________________________________________

SESSION THREE

# EARLY MINISTRY IN JERUSALEM AND SAMARIA

**Memory Verse: God is spirit, and those who worship Him must worship in spirit and truth (John 4:24 NASB).**

How many of us do things simply because it's the way we've always done them? Maybe it's the way we greet people or show affection. Maybe it's the church we go to or the traditions we celebrate. Most of the time, these rituals or traditions that color how we live life are good things. But often, if we don't examine the reasons why we do what we do, we can get caught in *doing* just for the sake of *doing*. And if this causes us to reject God's best for us or miss out on seeing the truth, then we have allowed tradition to take the place of real Christ-centered living.

It's so easy to fall into the trap of ritualism without remembering why we observe the traditions that we do. In this session we'll look at Jesus encountering two people—a man named Nicodemus and a Samaritan woman—who live by traditions that hinder them from understanding who Jesus is.

## Connecting

Open your group with prayer. It can be easy to let prayer become routine or ritualistic. Let's be careful to not just go through the motions but to truly come before God together as we begin this study.

1. Most people want to live a healthy, balanced life. A regular medical checkup is a good way to measure health and spot potential problems. In the same way, a spiritual checkup is vital to your spiritual well-being. The *Personal Health Assessment* was designed to give you a quick snapshot, or pulse, of your spiritual health. Take a few minutes individually to complete the *Personal Health Assessment.* After answering each question, tally your results.

2. Pair up with your spiritual partner and briefly share one purpose area from your *Personal Health Assessment* where you are strong and one that needs a little work. Share one step you would like to take this week to work on your spiritual health. Note this on your *Personal Health Plan.* Make a note about your partner's plans and how you can pray for him or her this week.

3. Share one thing that you do daily or nearly every day without fail. What do you think motivates your commitment to the activity?

## Growing

Early in Jesus's ministry he confirms through words and deeds that he is the Messiah who will provide renewal to Israel and inaugurate a new era of salvation through his life, death, and resurrection.

Read John 3:1–21.

4. A man named Nicodemus comes to Jesus by night. Who is he and why does he come (John 3:1–2)?

What do you think is significant about the time of day when Nicodemus visits?

5. How would you explain in your own words what Jesus says to Nicodemus in 3:3?

   What role does the Spirit of God have in what Jesus has come to do (3:4–8)?

6. Why do you think Nicodemus has so much trouble understanding Jesus, even though he's a leader and teacher, undoubtedly steeped in the Scriptures (3:4, 9–10)?

7. How does John summarize Jesus's mission in 3:16–17?

8. Nicodemus comes at night, avoiding the light. Light and darkness are themes in 1:4–9, and they return in 3:19–21. In these verses, what do people who hate the light do? Why?

   What do people who love the light do? Why?

Read John 4:1–42. See the *Study Notes* for background on the Samaritans.

9. With Nicodemus, Jesus uses the metaphor of birth to explain what he is offering. With the Samaritan woman, he uses the metaphor of water. How does he get this woman more and more interested in the "water" he offers (4:4–26)?

   In what ways is water a good description of what Jesus offers (4:13)?

10. Why do you think it takes so long for this woman to understand and embrace what Jesus is saying?

11. Jesus's insight into this woman's life, and his revelation that he is the Messiah, eventually cause her to take action despite her poor reputation. Compare John 4:28–30 with John 4:39–42.

How does the woman respond to her conversation with Jesus, and what is the result?

12. As you look at your own response to Jesus, who have you been more like:
    - ☐ like Nicodemus, who has trouble understanding and connecting with Jesus despite his training in the Bible (3:4, 9–10)
    - ☐ like the scorned, sinful Samaritan woman who is mistrustful at first but then embraces with abandon what Jesus offers and tells others about him
    - ☐ like neither of them (please explain)

13. What response do you think Jesus is asking of you today?

Jesus's clearing of the temple and his discussions with Nicodemus and the Samaritan woman further establish that he is the Messiah bringing salvation to all. This salvation will involve transformation and purification brought about by the Holy Spirit.

## Developing

One way to avoid the trap of ritualism and begin to worship in spirit and in truth is by serving others in the body of Christ. God often provides service opportunities to open our eyes to truths we might not otherwise see.

14. Discuss some of the many ways that we can serve the body of Christ. Is there a particular area of service that God has put on your heart to serve either this group or in your local church? If not, investigate the opportunities and pray about finding a ministry in which you can serve. As you take that first step, God will lead you to the ministry that expresses your passion.

15. Spending time getting to know each other outside of group meetings is helpful to building stronger relationships within

your group. Discuss whether your group would like to have a potluck or other type of social to celebrate together what God is doing in your group. You could plan to share a meal prior to a small group meeting or plan to follow your completion of this study with a barbecue. Appoint one or two people who can follow up with everyone outside of group time to put a plan together.

## Sharing

Many people believe all religions worship the same God, only the customs or rituals are different. But Jesus is not about keeping rituals. In fact, Jesus often reprimanded the religious leaders, saying, "Why do you break the command of God for the sake of your tradition?" (Matt. 15:3 NIV). Jesus's desire is for all to come to know him in personal relationship.

16. In the last session you were asked to write some names in the *Circles of Life* diagram. Have you followed up with those you identified who need to connect with other Christians? If not, when will you contact them? Go back to the *Circles of Life* to remind yourself of the various people you come into contact with on a regular basis. Pray for an opportunity to approach them this week.

17. Today we learned about Jesus's compelling encounter and subsequent conversion of the Samaritan woman. Jesus desires to compel each of us to make the life-changing decision to accept his gift of salvation. If any part of our study so far has encouraged you and you have never invited Jesus to take control of your life, why not ask him now? If you are not clear about God's gift of eternal life for everyone who believes in Jesus and how to receive this gift, take a minute to pray and ask God to help you understand what he wants you to do about trusting in Jesus.

## Surrendering

Small groups are a great place to learn the importance of remaining transparent in our lives and it begins by sharing our spiritual journeys with each other.

18. Take some time now to begin the Circle of Prayer exercise. This exercise allows for focused prayer over each person or couple in the group. Each person or couple will have an opportunity to share any pressing needs, concerns, or struggles requiring prayer, and the rest of the group will pray for these requests. More complete instructions for this can be found in the *Leader's Notes*.

19. Have one person close this session in prayer, making sure to thank God for all he's done in and through your group to this point.

## Study Notes

***Samaritans:*** The Samaritans were descended from the inhabitants of the northern kingdom after Israel divided. After the Assyrians conquered the northern kingdom, many Israelites were taken captive and deported. The Assyrians brought in colonists who intermarried with the remaining inhabitants. Samaritans were therefore considered to be a mixed race. When the Jews who returned from Babylonian captivity refused the Samaritans' help to rebuild the temple, the hostility turned deadly. The old bitterness between the northern and southern kingdoms no doubt intensified matters. By the time of Christ, the animosity hadn't lessened. Jews from Galilee who wanted to reach Jerusalem went out of their way to avoid Samaria. "You are a Samaritan and have a demon" was a common insult (see John 8:48 for an example). To make matters worse, this Samaritan was a female of low virtue, and no respectable Jewish man would talk with a woman in public.

***Living Water:*** In Jeremiah 2:13, God calls himself "the fountain of living water." In Ezekiel 47:9 and Zechariah 14:8, the Old Testament prophets look forward to a time when living water would flow out of Jerusalem. John applies this to Jesus in reference to the eternal life he offers. In John 7:38–39, Jesus links this water to the Holy Spirit.

***Mount Gerizim:*** Both the Samaritans and the Jews acknowledged that God had designated places of worship to their forefathers. The Jews understood this place to be the temple in Jerusalem. The Samaritans embraced only the books of Genesis through Deuteronomy and believed that the mountain on which Abraham built the altar at Shechem was overlooked by Mount Gerizim. For this reason, they chose Mount Gerizim as their special place of worship.

## For Deeper Study (Optional)

1. John 2:24–25 is interesting in that it comes right after many people believe in Jesus because of his signs. What does this reveal to us about Jesus's knowledge of people and of his purpose on earth?

2. Compare the woman's response in John 4:25–29 to Nicodemus's in John 3:2–9. How do their responses prove that learning and education can sometimes hinder a person's ability to see truth?

## Reflections

If you've been spending time each day connecting with God through his Word, congratulations! Some experts say that it takes twenty-one repetitions to develop a new habit. By the end of this week, you'll be well on your way to cultivating new spiritual habits that will encourage you in your walk with God. This week, continue to read the daily verses, giving prayerful consideration to what you learn about God, his Spirit, and his place in your life. Then, as before, record your thoughts, insights, or prayers in the space provided. On the sixth day, record a summary of what you have learned throughout the week.

***Day 1.*** For zeal for your house consumes me, and the insults of those who insult you fall on me (Ps. 69:9 NIV).

REFLECT

______________________________________________

______________________________________________

______________________________________________

______________________________________________

***Day 2.*** What this means is that those who become Christians become new persons. They are not the same anymore, for the old life is gone. A new life has begun! (2 Cor. 5:17 NLT).

REFLECT

______________________________________________

______________________________________________

______________________________________________

______________________________________________

***Day 3.*** For you have been born again. Your new life did not come from your earthly parents because the life they gave you will end in death. But this new life will last forever because it comes from the eternal, living word of God (1 Peter 1:23 NLT).

REFLECT

______________________________________________

______________________________________________

______________________________________________

______________________________________________

*Day 4.* And I will give you a new heart with new and right desires, and I will put a new spirit in you. I will take out your stony heart of sin and give you a new, obedient heart. And I will put my Spirit in you so you will obey my laws and do whatever I command (Ezek. 36:26–27 NLT).

REFLECT

______________________________________________

______________________________________________

______________________________________________

______________________________________________

*Day 5.* The Spirit and the bride say, "Come!" And let him who hears say, "Come!" Whoever is thirsty, let him come; and whoever wishes, let him take the free gift of the water of life (Rev. 22:17 NIV).

REFLECT

______________________________________________

______________________________________________

______________________________________________

______________________________________________

*Day 6.* Record your weekly summary of what God has shown you in the space below.

SUMMARY

______________________________________________

______________________________________________

______________________________________________

______________________________________________

SESSION FOUR

# MORE SIGNS AND MIRACLES FROM THE MESSIAH

**Memory Verse: Then Jesus declared, "I am the bread of life. He who comes to me will never go hungry, and he who believes in me will never be thirsty" (John 6:35 NIV).**

Throughout the book of John, Jesus performed many signs and wonders. He changed ordinary water into wine. He healed a royal official's son and an invalid at the pool of Bathesda. He fed five thousand families with just five barley loaves and two small fish. He walked on water, and more.

Throughout history, many people have tried to explain the mysteries of God through science and reason. But a miracle explained by any reason other than God is no miracle at all. There is no explanation needed except that in performing signs and wonders, Jesus confirmed he is the one and only, Son of God and Messiah in whom we can have assurance of our salvation.

## Connecting

Open your group with prayer. Thank God for revealing himself to us through Jesus.

1. Take five minutes to check in with your spiritual partner, or with another partner if yours is absent. Turn to your *Personal Health Plan*. Share with your partner how your time with God went this week. What is one thing you discovered? Or, what obstacles hindered you from following through? Make a note about your partner's progress and how you can pray for him or her.

2. When have you ever felt like there were things you should do but lacked the resources to accomplish them?

## Growing

Jesus continues to perform signs of compassion and power, signs that show his concern for people and his power over disease and the natural world. He wants people to respond by showing deeper interest in who he is. But often their response shows how spiritually blind they are.

3. Describe the healing Jesus performs in 5:1–15.

4. How do the Jewish leaders respond to this healing, and why (5:9–16)?

5. In response to the charge that he has violated God's law of resting on the Sabbath, Jesus makes a series of astonishing claims about himself (5:17–30). List the things he says about himself—his abilities and his relationship with God.

6. If these claims are true, what are the implications for your life? What should you think, feel, and do?

7. In 6:1–15, Jesus feeds a crowd as miraculously as the way Moses fed the Israelites with manna and quail in the desert (Exodus 16; Numbers 11). How do the people respond (John 6:14–15)?

   Do you think this is the response Jesus wants? Explain.

8. In 6:16–24, Jesus further demonstrates his complete power over the natural world by walking on water. When you think about these signs—healing the sick, feeding the hungry, walking on water—how do you respond?

   ☐ I wish Jesus would do something like that for me.

   ☐ I have trouble believing in this supernatural stuff.

   ☐ I am moved by Jesus's compassion for ordinary people.

   ☐ I want to talk about Jesus to those who don't believe in him, even if I'm rejected the way he was.

   ☐ I __________.

9. Jesus explains some of the response he wants in the following verses. In each case, what does he ask people to do in response to his works?

   ☐ 6:26–29

   ☐ 6:35–36

   ☐ 6:48–57

10. What do you think it means to eat Jesus's flesh and drink his blood (6:53)?

11. What are some of the things people try to feed their bodies and souls with, other than Jesus?

    How can you feed on Jesus as the bread of life this week?

Jesus continues to show that he is the one sent from God, uniquely related to the Father as his Son, equal with the Father yet submitted to him. Many reject his uncompromising claims, yet we know that he is the one who supplies the bread of life, that he takes care of our physical needs and even our spiritual hunger and thirst.

## Developing

Jesus gave us the example of meeting people's physical needs so they would be able to listen to his spiritual teachings.

12. Brainstorm some ways you as a group can meet someone's physical needs. Consider collecting items for a local crisis pregnancy center. Maybe you know of an elderly person who could use help with some household chores or yard work. You best know the needs of your neighbors and community. Commit to picking a project and a date by next week.

13. The Bible reveals the many spiritual gifts given to believers. Take time to review the *Spiritual Gifts Inventory* in the *Appendix*. Discuss which of the listed gifts you believe you may have.

    Once you have an idea about what your spiritual gifts are, discuss how your specific gift(s) might meet a need within your small group. For example, the gift of administration might meet the need to keep the roster updated; or the gift of hospitality might be used to plan a group social activity.

## Sharing

Sometimes sharing the Bread of Life and the Living Water is best done over a cup of coffee or a meal. Keep that in mind as you follow through with the people in your *Circles of Life*.

14. If you are having trouble following through on your commitment to share with the people in your *Circles of Life*, pray right now for God's enabling power. Then, make a commitment to take the next step this week. Enlist your spiritual partner to pray for you and hold you accountable to your goals.

15. Telling your own story is a powerful way to share Jesus with others. Turn to *Telling Your Story* in the *Appendix*. Review this with your spiritual partner. Begin developing your story by taking a few minutes to share briefly what your life was like before you knew Christ. (If you haven't yet committed your life to Christ or are not sure, you can find information about this in the *Sharing* section of *Session Three*. If you became a Christian at a very young age and don't remember what life was like before Christ, reflect on what you have seen in the life of someone close to you.) Make notes about this aspect of your story below and commit to writing it out this week. Then, spend some time individually developing your complete story using the *Telling Your Story* exercise in the *Appendix*.

______________________________________________

______________________________________________

______________________________________________

**Surrendering**

Beyond our physical needs, God meets all our spiritual needs as well. How has God satisfied your hunger and thirst? How has he met your needs?

16. Several people share with the group how God has met your spiritual needs.

17. Last week you began praying for the specific needs of each person or couple in the group during the Circle of Prayer exercise. Take some time now to pray over those for whom the group hasn't yet prayed. As you did last week, allow each individual to share whatever specific needs or challenges they are facing. Then have that person stand, sit, or kneel in the middle of the room. Join hands around them, or place your hands on their shoulders if everyone is comfortable doing that, and take turns praying for the specific needs shared. Ask for God's transforming power to bring change to the situations at hand.

## For Deeper Study (Optional)

1. In John 5:5–8 there is an interesting conversation between Jesus and the sick man. Jesus asks him a question in verse 6. How does the man respond?

2. How is this like the excuses we often use for not improving our spiritual health? How does Jesus respond to the man's excuses?

## Reflections

Second Timothy 3:16–17 reads, "All Scripture is God-breathed and is useful for teaching, rebuking, correcting and training in righteousness, so that the man of God may be thoroughly equipped for every good work" (NIV). Allow God's Word to train you in righteousness as you read, reflect on, and respond to the Scripture in your daily time with God this week.

***Day 1.*** Then the LORD said to Moses, "Look, I'm going to rain down food from heaven for you. The people can go out each day and pick up as much food as they need for that day. I will test them in this to see whether they will follow my instructions (Exod. 16:4 NLT).

REFLECT

___

___

___

___

*Day 2.* They asked, and He brought quail, and satisfied them with the bread of heaven (Ps. 105:40 NASB).

REFLECT

__________________________________________________________

__________________________________________________________

__________________________________________________________

__________________________________________________________

*Day 3.* On this mountain the LORD Almighty will prepare a feast of rich food for all peoples, a banquet of aged wine—the best of meats and the finest of wines (Isa. 25:6 NIV).

REFLECT

__________________________________________________________

__________________________________________________________

__________________________________________________________

__________________________________________________________

*Day 4.* He humbled you, causing you to hunger and then feeding you with manna, which neither you nor your fathers had known, to teach you that man does not live on bread alone but on every word that comes from the mouth of the LORD (Deut. 8:3 NIV).

REFLECT

__________________________________________________________

__________________________________________________________

__________________________________________________________

__________________________________________________________

***Day 5.*** I am the living bread that came down from heaven. If anyone eats of this bread, he will live forever. This bread is my flesh, which I will give for the life of the world (John 6:51 NIV).

REFLECT

______________________________________________________________________

______________________________________________________________________

______________________________________________________________________

______________________________________________________________________

***Day 6.*** Use the following space to record your summary of how God has challenged you this week.

SUMMARY

______________________________________________________________________

______________________________________________________________________

______________________________________________________________________

______________________________________________________________________

SESSION FIVE

# JESUS IN JERUSALEM FOR THE FEASTS OF TABERNACLES AND DEDICATION

**Memory Verse:** My sheep listen to my voice; I know them, and they follow me (John 10:27 NIV).

Phillip Keller wrote in his book *A Shepherd Looks at Psalm 23*, "The greater, the wider, the more majestic my concept is of the Christ—the more vital will be my relationship to him. Obviously, David, in this Psalm, is speaking not as the shepherd, though he was one, but as a sheep, one of the flock. He spoke with a strong sense of pride and devotion and admiration. It was as though he literally boasted aloud, 'Look at who my shepherd is—my owner—my manager!' The Lord is! After all, he knew from firsthand experience that the lot in life of any particular sheep depended on the type of man who owned it."*

At the time of Christ, a man could acquire a flock of sheep one of three ways. He could tend his father's flock, his father could give him a herd, or he could purchase a herd at a price. When Jesus talked to the disciples about being the Good Shepherd, they understood that Jesus had been given his Father's flock, the people of Israel. Jesus continued the close, caring relationship of a shepherd for his sheep, even laying down his life for the protection of his flock.

* Phillip Keller, *A Shepherd Looks at Psalm 23* (Grand Rapids: Zondervan, 1970), 17.

## Connecting

Open your group with prayer for open hearts and minds to hear the Good Shepherd's voice.

1. Check in with your spiritual partner, or with another partner if yours is absent. Talk about any challenges you are facing in reaching the goals you have set throughout this study. Tell your spiritual partner how he or she has helped you follow through with each step. Be sure to write down your partner's progress.

2. Sharing a meal is a great way to get to know the others in your group better. During *Session Three*, you should have discussed whether your group would like to have a potluck or social. Take a few minutes now to tie up any loose ends in your plan.

3. What is one of the biggest sacrifices you have ever made?

## Growing

Jesus continues to encounter opposition from the religious authorities as he teaches during the Jewish Feast of Tabernacles and Feast of Dedication. Through his teaching and miracles, he demonstrates that he is the fulfillment of the promises celebrated by Israel's feasts. See the *Study Notes* for more information on the feasts.

In chapters 7, Jesus goes to the temple during the Feast of Tabernacles. A debate erupts over who he is, with the citizens of Jerusalem, the crowd that has traveled there for the feast, the religious leaders, and the temple guards arguing among themselves.

4. Water is one of the main symbols in the Feast of Tabernacles. How does Jesus use this symbol to explain his identity in 7:37–39?

   Would you describe your experience of the Holy Spirit as "rivers of living water?" Please explain.

5. Another of the main symbols at the Feast of Tabernacles is light. How does Jesus employ that symbol in 8:2?

   What do you think it means to say that whoever follows Jesus will never walk in darkness?

Read John 9.

6. What is Jesus's explanation for the man's blindness (9:3–5)?

   Have you ever seen God use a disability or weakness and turn it into something that glorifies him? If so, when?

7. The story in John 9 is mainly about spiritual sight and blindness, which are related to loving the light or preferring darkness. In the following verses, trace the blind man's progress toward having more and more sight.

   - ☐ 9:6–12
   - ☐ 9:13–17
   - ☐ 9:25
   - ☐ 9:30–38

8. How do the Pharisees repeatedly choose spiritual darkness or blindness in this story (see 9:13–19, 24–34, 39–41, especially vv. 16, 24, and 29)?

9. John's record of the healing of the man born blind is his sixth of the seven miracles, or signs, that John recounts to confirm Jesus as Messiah. How does Jesus's sixth miracle give additional evidence that he was the Son of God?

10. Was there ever a time in your life when you clung to spiritual blindness, perhaps even despite evidence that you were wrong? If so, why did you do that?

11. Have you had the humbling experience of admitting you were blind and didn't know much about Jesus? If so, what was that like, and what was the result? Did it lead to more sight?

12. How can you treat Jesus as the light of the world? For instance, do you need to pursue more light? Do you need to stand up for the truth?

Jesus's teaching and healing at the Feast of Tabernacles confirm that he is the Messiah, the source of living water and true light. Like the various people who encounter him at the feast, we too need to decide each day whether to humble ourselves to receive his water and light, or whether to choose the blindness of seeing things our way.

**Developing**

During previous sessions, we've discussed how God has given every believer spiritual gifts to serve him within the body of Christ and how to translate those gifts into ministry to our small group.

13. This week, discuss how you may be able to use your gifts to serve beyond this small group to the ministries in your church and plan to get involved in serving the body of Christ right away. It's amazing to experience God using you to fill a specific need within his church.

14. On your *Personal Health Plan*, next to the "Develop" icon,
ou serving?" question. If you are
e area where you will consider
g for the right opportunity and

e reactions to Jesus were mixed.
him. But that still doesn't relieve

us of our responsibility to share Jesus with others. As we are faithful to share with others, we can trust the Holy Spirit to work in their hearts to evoke change.

15. In *Session Two*, you identified people within your *Circles of Life* that needed connection to Christian community. Jesus's commission in Acts 1:8 says, "But you will receive power when the Holy Spirit comes on you; and you will be my witnesses in Jerusalem, and in all Judea and Samaria, and to the ends of the earth" (NIV). Jesus intended his followers to share him not only within our own circles of influence (our Jerusalem), but also in Judea and Samaria, and the ends of the earth. Judea included the region in which Jerusalem was located. Today, this includes our neighboring communities or cities. As a group, discuss the following possible actions you can take to share Jesus with your Judea in a tangible way.

    - ☐ Collect children's books or school supplies to donate to needy schools in a nearby community.
    - ☐ Donate basic personal care items to a local convalescent home or assisted care facility for the elderly. Plan to deliver the items together and spend an hour or two visiting with lonely residents.
    - ☐ Contact your local mission or homeless shelter and ask how your group might be able to volunteer. Some offer opportunities to donate handwritten holiday or birthday cards that they give to their residents.

## Surrendering

Understanding Jesus as our Good Shepherd, the one who loves us and protects us to the point of laying down his life for us can be a powerful new way to look at our relationship with him.

16. Have someone volunteer to read Psalm 23 out loud while the rest of the group considers it in light of what it means to be sheep under the care of the Good Shepherd.

17. During the past two weeks, you've been praying for the specific needs of each person or couple in the group during the Circle of Prayer exercise. Take some time now to pray over those for whom the group hasn't yet prayed. As you did last week, allow each individual to share whatever specific needs or challenges they are facing. Ask for God's transforming power to bring change to their lives.

18. Don't forget to share your praises and prayer requests with one another and conclude your group time in prayer.

## Study Notes

***Feast of Tabernacles:*** Also called Feast of Booths. The Feast of Tabernacles was a celebration of the grape and olive harvest and commemorated God's faithfulness during the period of the desert wanderings. This celebration, which began on the fifteenth of the seventh month of the Jewish calendar (sometime during September–October), was the most popular of the three main Jewish feasts (Passover, Pentecost, and Tabernacles). The feast was known for the shelters (booths or tabernacles) created from palm and willow trees that the Jews would live in during the seven-day festival. Also important at the feast were water-drawing and lamp-lighting rites, to which Jesus refers in John 7:37–38; 8:12; and 9:5.

***Pharisees:*** The Pharisees were a religious party who held to a strict interpretation of the law of Moses as well as a large body of oral interpretations of the law and the rest of the Bible. They were mainly laymen, and there weren't many of them, but they were widely respected for living godly lives and knowing the Bible well.

## For Deeper Study (Optional)

The testimony theme runs throughout the book of John. In this section Jesus testifies that he is the light of the world. Compare this with other testimonies in 3:31–36; 5:31–47; and 10:1–18.

1. What does Jesus say about the value of testimonies, actions, and Scripture working together?

2. What lesson should we take from this when evaluating teachings or claims?

## Reflections

The Lord promised Joshua success and prosperity in Joshua 1:8 when he said, “Do not let this Book of the Law depart from your mouth; meditate on it day and night, so that you may be careful to do everything written in it. Then you will be prosperous and successful” (NIV). We too can claim this promise for our lives as we commit to meditate on the Word of God each day. As in previous weeks, read and meditate on the daily verses and record any prayers or insights you gain in the space provided. Summarize what you have learned this week on Day 6.

***Day 1.*** Then we your people, the sheep of your pasture, will thank you forever and ever, praising your greatness from generation to generation (Ps. 79:13 NLT).

REFLECT

________________________________________

________________________________________

________________________________________

________________________________________

***Day 2.*** For he is our God. We are the people he watches over, the sheep under his care. Oh, that you would listen to his voice today! (Ps. 95:7 NLT).

REFLECT

---

---

---

---

***Day 3.*** Know that the LORD Himself is God; It is He who has made us, and not we ourselves; We are His people and the sheep of His pasture (Ps. 100:3 NASB).

REFLECT

---

---

---

---

***Day 4.*** My people have been lost sheep; their shepherds have led them astray and caused them to roam on the mountains. They wandered over mountain and hill and forgot their own resting place (Jer. 50:6 NIV).

REFLECT

---

---

---

---

***Day 5.*** All of us have strayed away like sheep. We have left God's paths to follow our own. Yet the LORD laid on him the guilt and sins of us all (Isa. 53:6 NLT).

REFLECT

___

___

___

___

***Day 6.*** Use the following space to write any thoughts God has put in your heart and mind during *Session Five* and your *Reflections* time this week.

SUMMARY

___

___

___

___

SESSION SIX

# RAISING LAZARUS AND COMING TO JERUSALEM

**Memory Verse:** **The next day the great crowd that had come for the Feast heard that Jesus was on his way to Jerusalem. They took palm branches and went out to meet him, shouting, "Hosanna! Blessed is he who comes in the name of the Lord! Blessed is the King of Israel!" (John 12:12–13 NIV).**

Much truth can be found within the lines of Benjamin Franklin's epitaph, penned at the age of twenty-two. It reads as follows:

The Body of
B. Franklin, Printer.
Like the Cover of an old Book
Its contents torn out,
And stript of its Lettering and Guilding,
Lies here, Food for Worms,
But the Work shall not be wholly lost:
For it will, as he believ'd,
Appear once more
In a new and more perfect Edition,
Corrected and amended by the Author.*

* H. W. Brands, *The First American: The Life and Times of Benjamin Franklin* (New York: Anchor Books, 2002).

Our bodies on earth are temporary and subject to damage and injury. When we die our bodies will decay, but in heaven we will receive new and more perfect editions, corrected and amended by our author.

In *Session Six* we see how Jesus used the very essence of humanity, our physical bodies, to prove he was God. He allowed his dear friend Lazarus's earthly body to get sick to the point of death and decay so he could restore him to life as the ultimate proof that he was the Son of God and Messiah.

## Connecting

Open your group with prayer and invite the Holy Spirit to guide you through your study time.

1. Check in with your spiritual partner, or with another partner if yours is absent. Share your progress and any challenges you are currently facing. Take a few minutes to pray for each other now.

2. What spiritually related news headline has gotten your attention recently? Discuss why it attracted your attention.

## Growing

The raising of Lazarus from the dead is the climax of the signs Jesus gives to demonstrate that he is the Son of God, and it's a prelude to his display of power at his own resurrection. However, the threat of death hangs over this chapter. Some of Jesus's countrymen have tried multiple times to stone him for blasphemy, because he has claimed to be God (8:57–59; 10:29–33, 39). Bethany is near Jerusalem, and even Jesus's disciples know how dangerous it will be for him to go there.

Please read John 11 aloud.

3. Jesus loves Lazarus, yet he waits two days to go see him when he hears Lazarus is sick. Note the explanation Jesus offers for

his delay (11:4). How is it like and unlike the explanation he gave for the blind man's blindness (9:3)?

Do you think it's common for God to allow people to suffer so that ultimately God can display his glory through the situation? Explain.

4. Mary and Martha each meet Jesus before he reaches the house. Martha reaches him first. What faith in Jesus does Martha express in 11:20–27?

   Do you think Jesus wants more faith from her than that? Please explain.

5. If what Jesus says in 11:25–26 is true, what are the implications for you personally? How does this affect the way you live your life?

6. The raising of Lazarus is a turning point. Such a sign of power demands either faith for those who choose the light (11:45) or a determination to kill Jesus for those who claim they can see but who really live in darkness (11:46–57). What reasons do the leaders in Jerusalem give for deciding to kill Jesus rather than embrace him (11:47–49)?

   What do you think of their reasons?

7. Read John 12:1–8. Before the Passover, Jesus attends a dinner at the home of Mary, Martha, and Lazarus. What does Mary do at this dinner (v. 3)?

   What do you think prompts her emotional and lavish act?

8. Jesus treats Mary's behavior as neither sexually nor financially inappropriate (12:7–8). What does that say about him?

9. Is Mary a model for us? If so, how? If not, why not?

Read John 12:12–21.

10. "Hosanna" (12:13) means "Save us now!" The crowd is quoting Psalm 118:25–26 to greet the man who can raise the dead and who, therefore, must be the Messiah King who will liberate them from the Romans. How do you think they will feel when they find out that he doesn't plan to take up arms against the hated Romans?

11. Zechariah 9:9 says, "Rejoice greatly, O Daughter of Zion! Shout, Daughter of Jerusalem! See, your king comes to you, righteous and having salvation, gentle and riding on a donkey, on a colt, the foal of a donkey" (NIV). How does Jesus fulfill this prophecy (John 12:14–15)?

    A military Messiah would ride a war horse. Read Zechariah 9:9–10. What should the crowd learn from Jesus's choice of a donkey as a mount?

12. While his followers are celebrating, Jesus says that the hour has come for him to be "glorified" (12:23). What will reveal Jesus's glory (12:24–25)? Is it the crowd's shouts of praise?

    What does Jesus want us to learn from his example?

By raising Lazarus from the dead and then riding as a triumphal King into Jerusalem, Jesus puts the Jewish leaders into a position in which they must either acknowledge him as King or arrest him. He knows very well what is coming. Are we like those who cheer for him when things look good? Or are we willing to lay our lives on the line for him?

## Developing

Mary's anointing of Jesus is a beautiful example of service, which should inspire us to serve with hearts of humility.

13. To serve as Mary did, we need to be willing to humble ourselves to carry out even the most menial of tasks. This could mean

doing yard work, painting a house, or cleaning for someone who is in need. If time permits during this session, discuss with one another how you might serve a needy family in your church. Devise a game plan and then commit to seeing it through. You could choose one or two people who are willing to follow up with your church or a local ministry to put your plan into action.

14. If you've been spending time with God each day, consider journaling as a way to grow even closer to God. Read through *Journaling 101* in the *Appendix*. Commit this week to spending a portion of your time with God writing your thoughts and prayers in a journal.

15. Briefly discuss the future of your group. How many of you are willing to stay together as a group and work through another study together? Turn to the *Small Group Agreement* and talk about any changes you would like to make as you move forward as a group.

## Sharing

When Jesus raised Lazarus from the dead, many people became believers. Most of us have dead areas in our lives—relationships, hopes, dreams—that Jesus has restored and brought back to life.

16. Return to the *Circles of Life* diagram now. Outside each circle, write down one or two names of people you know who need to know Christ. Commit to praying for an opportunity to share Jesus with each of them. You may invite them to attend an outreach event with you or you may feel led to share the good news with him or her over coffee. Share your commitment with your spiritual partner. Pray together for God's Holy Spirit to give you the words to speak with boldness.

17. Telling your own story is a powerful way to share Jesus with others. Turn to *Telling Your Story* in the *Appendix*. Review this with your spiritual partner. Begin developing your story

by taking a few minutes to share briefly what your life was like before you knew Christ. (If you haven't yet committed your life to Christ or are not sure, you can find information about this in the *Sharing* section of *Session Three*. If you became a Christian at a very young age and don't remember what life was like before Christ, reflect on what you have seen in the life of someone close to you.) Make notes about this aspect of your story below and commit to writing it out this week. Then, spend some time individually developing your complete story using the *Telling Your Story* exercise in the *Appendix*.

________________________________________

________________________________________

________________________________________

18. On your *Personal Health Plan*, next to the "Sharing" icon, answer the "WHEN are you shepherding another person in Christ?" question.

### Surrendering

Just as the people worshiped Jesus and shouted "hosanna!" as he came into Jerusalem, we need to take regular time out to praise him for who he is.

19. Share your praises and prayer requests with one another. Record these on the *Prayer and Praise Report*. Then end your time by praying for each other.

## For Deeper Study (Optional)

Compare Martha's conversation with Jesus in John 11:24–27 to 11:39–40. What changes Martha's perspective? Is it a matter of the difference between head knowledge and the actual application of faith? Why or why not?

## Reflections

J. Hudson Taylor once said, "Do not have your concert first, and then tune your instruments afterwards. Begin the day with the Word of God and prayer, and get first of all into harmony with Him."* Get into harmony with God as you spend time with him this week. Read and reflect on the daily verses. Then record your thoughts, insights, or prayers in the Reflect sections that follow. On the sixth day record your summary of what God has taught you this week.

*Day 1.* Blessed is he who comes in the name of the LORD. From the house of the LORD we bless you (Ps. 118:26 NIV).

REFLECT

________________________________________

________________________________________

________________________________________

________________________________________

*Day 2.* Rejoice greatly, O people of Zion! Shout in triumph, O people of Jerusalem! Look, your king is coming to you. He is righteous and victorious, yet he is humble, riding on a donkey—even on a donkey's colt (Zech. 9:9 NLT).

REFLECT

________________________________________

________________________________________

________________________________________

________________________________________

*Day 3.* For the LORD will remove his hand of judgment and will disperse the armies of your enemy. And the LORD himself, the King of Israel, will live among you! At last your troubles will be over, and you will fear disaster no more (Zeph. 3:15 NLT).

* Charlie Jones and Bob Kelly, *The Tremendous Power of Prayer: A Collection of Quotes and Inspirational Thoughts to Inspire Your Prayer Life* (West Monroe, LA: Howard Books, 2000).

REFLECT

*Day 4.* I am the living one who died. Look, I am alive forever and ever! And I hold the keys of death and the grave (Rev. 1:18 NLT).

REFLECT

*Day 5.* For to this end Christ died and lived again, that He might be Lord both of the dead and of the living (Rom. 14:9 NASB).

REFLECT

*Day 6.* Record your summary of what God has taught you this week.

SUMMARY

SESSION SEVEN

# THE LAST SUPPER AND THE FAREWELL DISCOURSE

**Memory Verse: If I then, the Lord and the Teacher, washed your feet, you also ought to wash one another's feet (John 13:14 NASB).**

Mother Teresa has been attributed with saying, "I am not sure exactly what heaven will be like, but I do know that when we die and it comes time for God to judge us, He will *not* ask, 'How many good things have you done in your life?' rather He will ask, 'How much *love* did you put into what you did?'"

Jesus didn't humbly wash his disciples feet during the Last Supper because he felt like doing something kind or because he felt it was required of him; he truly loved his disciples and wanted to demonstrate with his selfless actions the depth of his love. In so doing, he showed them, and believers today, how to live out lives of unselfish love for one another in even the most mundane of circumstances.

## Connecting

Open your group with prayer and prepare to focus on Jesus's final hours before his death.

1. Check in with your spiritual partner, or with another partner if yours is absent. Share your progress and any challenges you are currently facing. Consider checking in by e-mail or phone throughout the week if you both would like to. Take a few minutes to pray for each other now. Write down your partner's progress.

2. Share a time when you have been served in a way that made you feel humbled.

## Growing

During the first twelve chapters of the Gospel of John, Jesus's focus has been on ministry to the unbelieving nation. Beginning in chapter 13, however, as his public ministry comes to an end, he devotes his time entirely to his disciples.

Please read John 13:1–17, as well as the *Study Notes* on foot-washing.

3. What explanation for Jesus's decision to wash his disciples' feet does John give in 13:3–5?

   What motivation does Jesus give in 13:12–17?

4. What would it look like for you to follow Jesus's example?

5. Why does Peter react to the foot-washing as he does (13:6–10)?

6. In verses 8 and 10, Jesus implies that the washing has a deeper meaning than just the removal of physical dirt. What might Jesus be talking about here?

7. Why do you think it is sometimes difficult for us to let someone else serve us?

Read John 13:18–30.

8. After Jesus has washed everyone's feet, including Judas's, Judas does the very opposite of servanthood. What do you think is the significance of the phrase, "it was night" (13:30)?

Read John 13:31–38.

9. After Judas leaves, Jesus gives his most important command to his disciples (13:34–35). Why does he say it's so vital for them to obey this command?

   The command to love others is as old as Leviticus (Lev. 19:18). What is new is "as I have loved you." How does this phrase explain what love involves?

10. Jesus prepares his disciples for his departure with a long teaching in John 14–16. Among the many crucial things he wants them to understand is that he has to leave in order for the Father to send his Holy Spirit to them. In the following verses, what does Jesus promise the Spirit will do for the disciples?

    ☐ 14:15–17

    ☐ 14:26

    ☐ 16:7–15

11. What are some ways we experience these actions of the Holy Spirit today?

12. In John 15:1–7, Jesus says the key to living a fruitful life is to abide in him the way a branch abides in a vine. What do you think it means to "abide" in Christ?

    What kinds of fruit (15:8) do you think we will bear if we abide in him?

Jesus's farewell discourse prepares the disciples for servant leadership after Jesus's departure and promises them the gift of the Holy Spirit as an empowering, guiding and protecting presence in their lives. This gift of the Holy Spirit is available to believers today as we walk with Christ daily.

## Developing

Jesus's example of servanthood began with his disciples. In the same way, we can often get our feet wet by serving within our own small group or church.

13. First Corinthians 12:7 says, "A spiritual gift is given to each of us as a means of helping the entire church" (NLT). Review the *Spiritual Gifts Inventory* in the *Appendix* once again. If you haven't already done so, share what you believe your spiritual gifts are. If you have discovered a ministry in which to serve, share where you found the opportunities to exercise your gift(s), either within the small group, or in your church. This could serve as encouragement to those who are struggling to find a ministry.

    If you know your gifts but have not yet plugged into a ministry, discuss how your gifts might meet a need within your church. Make a commitment to take the necessary steps to get plugged into that ministry. Or if your group is continuing beyond this study of John, choose an area to begin serving within the small group.

    If you still do not know what your spiritual gifts are, review the inventory with a trusted friend who knows you well. Chances are they have witnessed one or more gifts in your life.

## Sharing

When Jesus prayed to the Father, he prayed that the disciples would be one so the world will believe the Father sent him. Unity, love, and service can be powerful witnesses in a mostly self-centered world.

14. How have acts of selflessness touched you? How have you used acts of selflessness to reach out to others?

15. During *Session Four* you discussed ways you as a group can meet someone's physical needs. If you brought items to donate tonight, spend a few minutes praying for the individuals or families who will receive them. If you have planned to serve in another way, finalize those plans now. Don't pass up the opportunity to serve the body of Christ in this tangible way.

### Surrendering

Jesus fully surrendered to the Father's will, even to the point of a terrible death. Most of us won't be asked to sacrifice nearly to that extent, but God does want our hearts completely.

16. Turn to the *Personal Health Plan* and individually consider the "HOW are you surrendering your heart?" question. Look to the *Sample Personal Health Plan* for help. Share some of your thoughts in the group.

17. Share your prayer requests and record them on the *Prayer and Praise Report*. Have any previous prayer requests been answered? If so, celebrate these answers to prayer. Then, in simple, one-sentence prayers, submit your requests to God and close by thanking God for his commitment to your relationship with him and how he has used this group to teach you more about faith.

## Study Notes

***Footwashing:*** The dirty roads of Palestine necessitated daily footwashing. Under normal circumstances, this would be done when one entered the house. The task was seen as demeaning and was reserved for the lowest servant. For a teacher to wash his disciples' feet was unheard of. It would provoke shock, not admiration.

## For Deeper Study (Optional)

As we learned today, we can only be successful spiritually if we "abide" in Christ, which means to remain in close fellowship with him.

1. What role does love play in "remaining" or "abiding" in Christ according to 1 John 4:4–21?

## Reflections

As you read the given verse each day, prayerfully consider what you learn about God, his Spirit, and his place in your life. Then record your thoughts, insights, or prayer in the *Reflect* section below the verses you read. On the sixth day record a summary of what you have learned over the entire week through this study.

***Day 1.*** Wash me clean from my guilt. Purify me from my sin (Ps. 51:2 NLT).

REFLECT

________________________________________

________________________________________

________________________________________

________________________________________

***Day 2.*** I will sprinkle clean water on you, and you will be clean; I will cleanse you from all your impurities and from all your idols (Ezek. 36:25 NIV).

REFLECT

---

---

---

---

***Day 3.*** Those who obey his commands live in him, and he in them. And this is how we know that he lives in us: We know it by the Spirit he gave us (1 John 3:24 NIV).

REFLECT

---

---

---

---

***Day 4.*** Live a life filled with love for others, following the example of Christ, who loved you and gave himself as a sacrifice to take away your sins. And God was pleased, because that sacrifice was like sweet perfume to him (Eph. 5:2 NLT).

REFLECT

---

---

---

---

***Day* 5.** No, in all these things we are more than conquerors through him who loved us. For I am convinced that neither death nor life, neither angels nor demons, neither the present nor the future, nor any powers, neither height nor depth, nor anything else in all creation, will be able to separate us from the love of God that is in Christ Jesus our Lord (Rom. 8:37–39 NIV).

REFLECT

________________________________________

________________________________________

________________________________________

________________________________________

***Day* 6.** Use the following space to summarize what God has revealed to you during *Session Seven* and the *Reflections*.

SUMMARY

________________________________________

________________________________________

________________________________________

________________________________________

SESSION EIGHT

# ARREST, TRIAL, CRUCIFIXION, AND RESURRECTION

**Memory Verse: She saw two angels in white sitting, one at the head, and one at the feet, where the body of Jesus had been lying (John 20:12 NASB).**

Harry Pritchett Jr. wrote a story entitled "Philip's Egg" for *Leadership Journal* in 1985. In the story a Sunday school teacher gave her children plastic eggs. She asked them to collect samples of "new life" as part of a lesson on Easter. When they brought the eggs back, gathered together, and opened them up, they discovered the typical symbols like a flower or a butterfly. Then they came to an egg with nothing inside. At first the children thought someone hadn't done the assignment correctly until the boy whose egg it was proudly pointed out, "The tomb is empty!"

As Philip knew, and the disciples would soon come to know, the empty tomb is the best symbol of new life there is.

## Connecting

Open your group with prayer and come together one last time for this session as we study the Lord's death and resurrection.

1. Take time in this final session to connect with your spiritual partner. What has God been showing you through these sessions about the life of Jesus? Check in with each other about the progress you have made in your spiritual growth during this study. Make plans about whether you will continue in your mentoring relationship outside your Bible study group.

2. Share one thing that you have discovered about God or something that has challenged or encouraged you during this study.

## Growing

In this final session we see the purpose of Jesus's life on earth: his death, resurrection, and exaltation, which conclusively demonstrate that he is Messiah and King.

3. After the Last Supper, Jesus and his disciples cross the Kidron Valley to a garden, where Judas meets them with a crowd of soldiers and officials. These arrest Jesus and take him before Annas, father-in-law of high priest Caiaphas. How does Jesus respond to being questioned (18:19–23)?

   What impression do you get of Jesus's emotions or frame of mind in this scene?

4. How would you compare Jesus's answers in this interrogation to Peter's in 18:15–18, 25–27?

   What are some situations in which we might find ourselves tempted to deny Jesus?

5. Annas sends Jesus to Caiaphas, who takes him to the Roman governor, Pilate (18:28–40). Again when interviewed, Jesus speaks with absolute confidence and control. What does he reveal about the nature of his kingship in 18:36–37?

   Do you think Jesus means that his kingship has nothing to do with this world? Please explain.

Read John 19:1–37. Though Pilate repeatedly declares Jesus innocent and wants to release him, he fears the Jewish leaders and agrees to crucify Jesus. See the *Study Notes* for more information on the Roman governorship.

6. Look at the following Old Testament passages concerning the Messiah and compare them to the corresponding verses in John to see how Scripture is fulfilled.

| Psalm 22:18 | John 19:24 |
|---|---|
| Psalm 69:21 | John 19:28–29 |
| Psalm 34:20; Exodus 12:46 | John 19:36 |
| Zechariah 12:10 | John 19:37 |

   Who is in control of this execution? How can you tell?

7. John 19:30 records Jesus's last words. What is the significance of his final statement? Look at the *Study Notes* for insight.

Read John 19:38–20:18. On Friday just before sunset, Joseph of Arimathea and Nicodemus take Jesus's body and place it in an expensive tomb, never before used. They wrap the body in linen along with an enormous quantity of powdered spices, enough for royal burial.

8. On Sunday morning before dawn, Mary Magdalene goes to the tomb and finds it empty. What are the significant events in 20:2–18? Why do you think they are significant?

9. Read John 20:19–23. Here Jesus begins to fulfill the many promises he has made about sending the Holy Spirit. How do you understand his words in 20:23?

10. In 20:30–31, John sums up what readers should take away from studying his Gospel. What reasons for believing that Jesus is the Messiah and Son of God have you found in John's Gospel?

God provided salvation and eternal life through the death, burial, resurrection, and exaltation of his Son for all who believe in him. What response is God asking of you?

## Developing

Whether you continue with this group or not, take the example of Christ's service with you to remind you to look for opportunities to serve others.

11. If your group still needs to make decisions about continuing to meet after this session, have that discussion now. Talk about what you will study, who will lead, and where and when you will meet.

    Review your *Small Group Agreement* and evaluate how well you met your goals. Discuss any changes you want to make as you move forward. As your group starts a new study, this is a great time to take on a new role or change roles of service in your group. What new role will you take on? If you are uncertain, maybe your group members have some ideas for you. Remember you aren't making a lifetime commitment to the new role; it will only be for a few weeks. Maybe someone would like to share a role with you if you don't feel ready to serve solo.

## Sharing

Jesus's final words to his disciples included instructions to go make disciples of others.

12. During the course of this study, you have made commitments to share Jesus with the people in your life, either by inviting your friends to grow in Christian community or by sharing the gospel in words or actions with unbelievers. Share with the group any highlights that you experienced as you stepped out in faith to share with others.

**Surrendering**

During Jesus's time on earth, he routinely took time apart to spend with his Father. One way to grow closer as a group is to worship the Father together in a meaningful way.

13. Close by praying for your prayer requests and take a couple of minutes to review the praises you have recorded over the past few weeks on the Prayer and Praise Report. Thank God for what he's done in your group during this study.

## Study Notes

***High Priest Roles:*** The office of high priest was supposed to be to be lifelong and hereditary. In addition to the regular duties as a priest, the high priest entered the Holy of Holies on the Day of Atonement to make atonement for the sins of the people. When he carried the breastplate inscribed with the names of the tribes of Israel, he acted as mediator between Israel and God. By the time of Jesus's earthly ministry, the high priest was the chief civil and ecclesiastical dignitary among the Jews. He was chairman of the Sanhedrin and head of the political relations with the Roman government. Rome had usurped the right to appoint the high priest, so it was no longer a lifelong office. Caiaphas was high priest, although his father-in-law, Annas (whom the Romans had deposed), retained much of his influence among the priestly families. For this reason Luke refers to both as "high priests" (Luke 3:2), and in John 18:13

Jesus is first taken to Annas before appearing before Caiaphas and the Sanhedrin.

***Roman Governorship:*** At the time of Jesus's birth, Herod the Great's sovereignty over the kingdom of Palestine was upheld by a Roman legion stationed at Jerusalem. In exchange, Herod paid tribute to the Roman government and provided auxiliaries for the Roman army. At Herod's death in 4 BC, the kingdom was divided between his three surviving sons, the largest portion falling to Archelaus, who ruled Judea, Samaria, and Idumea until AD 6, when the Romans deposed him. From then on, Roman procurators or governors ruled that part of Palestine, including Jerusalem. (Herod the Great's son—Herod Antipas—ruled Galilee, and we hear about him in passages like Luke 23:6–12.) Pontius Pilate was governor in AD 26–35. Although at times oppressive and heavy-handed, in general the Roman government displayed consideration for the religious scruples of the Jews. They were exempted from military service and the duty of appearing in court on the Sabbath. Temple worship was allowed to continue so long as loyalty to the emperor was maintained.

***It Is Finished:*** In the Greek this is just one word, *tetelestai*. "Receipts for taxes found in the papyri have written across them this single word, which means 'paid in full.' The price for our redemption from sin was paid in full by our Lord's death."

## Reflections

As you read through this final week of *Reflections*, prayerfully consider what God is showing you about his character, the Holy Spirit, and how he wants you to grow and change. Then, write down your thoughts or prayers in the space provided. Don't let this concluding week of *Reflections* be your last. Commit to continue reading, reflecting, and meditating on the Word of God daily. Use Day 6 to record your prayer of commitment to see this discipline become habit.

*Day 1.* You love him even though you have never seen him. Though you do not see him, you trust him; and even now you are happy with a glorious, inexpressible joy (1 Peter 1:8 NLT).

REFLECT

*Day 2.* For the Lamb in the center of the throne will be their shepherd, and will guide them to springs of the water of life; and God will wipe every tear from their eyes (Rev. 7:17 NASB).

REFLECT

*Day 3.* I myself no longer live, but Christ lives in me. So I live my life in this earthly body by trusting in the Son of God, who loved me and gave himself for me (Gal. 2:20 NLT).

REFLECT

***Day 4.*** For whenever you eat this bread and drink this cup, you proclaim the Lord's death until he comes (1 Cor. 11:26 NIV).

REFLECT

______________________________

______________________________

______________________________

______________________________

***Day 5.*** Dear brothers and sisters, you must be patient as you wait for the Lord's return. Consider the farmers who eagerly look for the rains in the fall and in the spring. They patiently wait for the precious harvest to ripen (James 5:7 NLT).

REFLECT

______________________________

______________________________

______________________________

______________________________

***Day 6.*** Use the following space to write your prayer of commitment to continue spending time daily in God's Word and prayer.

SUMMARY

______________________________

______________________________

______________________________

______________________________

APPENDIX

# FREQUENTLY ASKED QUESTIONS

**What do we do on the first night of our group?**

Like all fun things in life—have a party! A "get to know you" coffee, dinner, or dessert is a great way to launch a new study. You may want to review the *Small Group Agreement* and share the names of a few friends you can invite to join you. But most importantly, have fun before your study time begins.

**Where do we find new members for our group?**

This can be challenging, especially for new groups that have only a few people or for existing groups that lose a few people along the way. We encourage you to pray with your group and then brainstorm a list of people from work, church, your neighborhood, your children's school, family, the gym, and so forth. Then have each group member invite several of the people on his or her list. Another good strategy is to ask church leaders to make an announcement that your group is open to new members.

No matter how you find members, it's vital that you stay on the lookout for new people to join your group. All groups tend to go through healthy attrition—the result of moves, releasing new leaders, ministry opportunities, and so forth—and if the group gets too small, it could be at risk of shutting down. If you and your group stay open, you'll be amazed at the people God sends your way. The next person just might become a friend for life. You never know!

**How long will this group meet?**

It's totally up to the group—once you come to the end of this study. Most groups meet weekly for at least their first six months together, but every other week can work as well. We strongly recommend that the group meet for the first six months on a weekly basis if at all possible. This allows for continuity, and if people miss a meeting they aren't gone for a whole month.

At the end of this study, each group member may decide whether he or she wants to continue on for another study. Some groups launch relationships that last for years, and others are stepping-stones into another group experience. Either way, enjoy the journey.

**What if this group is not working for me?**

Personality conflicts, life stage differences, geographical distance, level of spiritual maturity, or any number of things can cause you to feel the group doesn't work for you. Relax. Pray for God's direction, and at the end of this study decide whether to continue with this group or find another. You don't buy the first car you look at or marry the first person you date, and the same goes with a group. Don't bail out before the study is finished—God might have something to teach you. Also, don't run from conflict or prejudge people before you have given them a chance. God is still working in you too!

**Who is the leader?**

Most groups have an official leader. But ideally, the group will mature and members will share the facilitation of meetings. We have discovered that healthy groups share hosting and leading of the group. This model ensures that all members grow, give their unique contribution, and develop their gifts. This study guide and the Holy Spirit can keep things on track even when you share leadership. Christ has promised to be in your midst as you gather. Ultimately, God is your leader each step of the way.

### How do we handle the child care needs in our group?

This can be a sensitive issue. We suggest that you empower the group to openly brainstorm solutions. You may try one option that works for a while and then adjust over time. Our favorite approach is for adults to meet in the living room or dining room, and share the cost of a babysitter (or two) who can be with the kids in a different part of the house. In this way, parents don't have to be away from their children all evening when their children are too young to be left at home. A second option is to use one home for the kids and a second home (close by) for the adults. A third idea is to rotate the responsibility of providing a lesson or care for the children either in the same home or in another home nearby. This can be an incredible blessing for kids. Finally, the most common idea is to decide that you need to have a night to invest in your spiritual lives individually or as a couple, and make your own arrangements for child care. No matter what decision the group makes, the best approach is to dialogue openly about both the problem and the solution.

# SMALL GROUP AGREEMENT

## Our Purpose

To transform our spiritual lives by cultivating our spiritual health in a healthy small group community. In addition, we:

______________________________

______________________________

______________________________

## Our Values

| | |
|---|---|
| **Group Attendance** | To give priority to the group meeting. We will call or e-mail if we will be late or absent. (Completing the *Small Group Calendar* will minimize this issue.) |
| **Safe Environment** | To help create a safe place where people can be heard and feel loved. (Please, no quick answers, snap judgments, or simple fixes.) |
| **Respect Differences** | To be gentle and gracious to people with different spiritual maturity, personal opinions, temperaments, or imperfections. We are all works in progress. |
| **Confidentiality** | To keep anything that is shared strictly confidential and within the group, and avoid sharing improper information about those outside the group. |
| **Encouragement for Growth** | To be not just takers but givers of life. We want to spiritually multiply our lives by serving others with our God-given gifts. |

| | |
|---|---|
| **Welcome for Newcomers** | To keep an open chair and share Jesus's dream of finding a shepherd for every sheep. |
| **Shared Ownership** | To remember that every member is a minister and to ensure that each attender will share a small team role or responsibility over time. (See the *Team Roles*.) |
| **Rotating Hosts/ Leaders and Homes** | To encourage different people to host the group in their homes, and to rotate the responsibility of facilitating each meeting. (See the *Small Group Calendar*.) |

## Our Expectations

- Refreshments/mealtimes ______________________________
- Child care ________________________________________
- When we will meet (day of week) ____________________
- Where we will meet (place) _________________________
- We will begin at (time) ________ and end at ___________
- We will do our best to have some or all of us attend a worship service together. Our primary worship service time will be __________
- Date of this agreement ______________________________
- Date we will review this agreement again _______________
- Who (other than the leader) will review this agreement at the end of this study ______________________________

# TEAM ROLES

The Bible makes clear that every member, not just the small group leader, is a minister in the body of Christ. In a healthy small group, every member takes on some small role or responsibility. It can be more fun and effective if you team up on these roles.

Review the team roles and responsibilities below, and have each member volunteer for a role or participate on a team. If someone doesn't know where to serve or is holding back, as a group, suggest a team or role. It's best to have one or two people on each team so you have each of the five purposes covered. Serving in even a small capacity will not only help your leader but also will make the group more fun for everyone. Don't hold back. Join a team!

The opportunities below are broken down by the five purposes and then by a *crawl* (beginning), *walk* (intermediate), or *run* (advanced) role. Try to cover at least the crawl and walk roles, and select a role that matches your group, your gifts, and your maturity.

**Team Roles** | **Team Player(s)**

**CONNECTING TEAM (Fellowship and Community Building)**

Crawl: Host a social event or group activity in the first week or two.

Walk: Create a list of uncommitted friends and then invite them to an open house or group social.

Run: Plan a twenty-four-hour retreat or weekend getaway for the group. Lead the *Connecting* time each week for the group.

**GROWING TEAM (Discipleship and Spiritual Growth)**

Crawl: Coordinate the spiritual partners for the group. Facilitate a three- or four-person discussion circle during the Bible study portion of your meeting. Coordinate the discussion circles.

Walk: Tabulate the *Personal Health Plans* in a summary to let people know how you're doing as a group. Encourage personal devotions through group discussions and pairing up with spiritual (accountability) partners.

Run: Take the group on a prayer walk, or plan a day of solitude, fasting, or personal retreat.

**SERVING TEAM (Discovering Your God-Given Design for Ministry)**

Crawl: Ensure that every member finds a group role or team he or she enjoys.

Walk: Have every member take a gift test and determine your group's gifts. Plan a ministry project together.

Run: Help each member decide on a way to use his or her unique gifts somewhere in the church.

**SHARING TEAM (Sharing and Evangelism)**

Crawl: Coordinate the group's *Prayer and Praise Report* of friends and family who don't know Christ.

Walk: Search for group mission opportunities and plan a cross-cultural group activity.

Run: Take a small group "vacation" to host a six-week group in your neighborhood or office. Then come back together with your current group.

**SURRENDERING TEAM (Surrendering Your Heart to Worship)**

Crawl: Maintain the group's *Prayer and Praise Report* or journal.

Walk: Lead a brief time of worship each week (at the beginning or end of your meeting).

Run: Plan a more unique time of worship.

# SMALL GROUP CALENDAR

Planning and calendaring can help ensure the greatest participation at every meeting. At the end of each meeting, review this calendar. Be sure to include a regular rotation of host homes and leaders, and don't forget birthdays, socials, church events, holidays, and mission/ministry projects.

| Date | Lesson | Dessert/Meal | Role |
|---|---|---|---|
| | | | |
| | | | |
| | | | |
| | | | |
| | | | |
| | | | |
| | | | |
| | | | |
| | | | |
| | | | |
| | | | |
| | | | |
| | | | |

# PERSONAL HEALTH ASSESSMENT

| | Just Beginning | Getting Going | Well Developed |
|---|---|---|---|

**CONNECTING with God's Family**

| | |
|---|---|
| I am deepening my understanding of and friendship with God in community with others. | 1 2 3 4 5 |
| I am growing in my ability both to share and to show my love to others. | 1 2 3 4 5 |
| I am willing to share my real needs for prayer and support from others. | 1 2 3 4 5 |
| I am resolving conflict constructively and am willing to forgive others. | 1 2 3 4 5 |
| CONNECTING Total | _____ |

**GROWING to Be Like Christ**

| | |
|---|---|
| I have a growing relationship with God through regular time in the Bible and in prayer (spiritual habits). | 1 2 3 4 5 |
| I am experiencing more of the characteristics of Jesus Christ (love, patience, gentleness, courage, self-control, etc.) in my life. | 1 2 3 4 5 |
| I am avoiding addictive behaviors (food, television, busyness, and the like) to meet my needs. | 1 2 3 4 5 |
| I am spending time with a Christian friend (spiritual partner) who celebrates and challenges my spiritual growth. | 1 2 3 4 5 |
| GROWING Total | _____ |

| | Just Beginning / Getting Going / Well Developed |
|---|---|
| **DEVELOPING Your Gifts to Serve Others** | |
| I have discovered and am further developing my unique God-given design. | 1 2 3 4 5 |
| I am regularly praying for God to show me opportunities to serve him and others. | 1 2 3 4 5 |
| I am serving in a regular (once a month or more) ministry in the church or community. | 1 2 3 4 5 |
| I am a team player in my small group by sharing some group role or responsibility. | 1 2 3 4 5 |
| DEVELOPING Total | _____ |
| **SHARING Your Life Mission Every Day** | |
| I am cultivating relationships with non-Christians and praying for God to give me natural opportunities to share his love. | 1 2 3 4 5 |
| I am praying and learning about where God can use me and our group cross-culturally for missions. | 1 2 3 4 5 |
| I am investing my time in another person or group who needs to know Christ. | 1 2 3 4 5 |
| I am regularly inviting unchurched or unconnected friends to my church or small group. | 1 2 3 4 5 |
| SHARING Total | _____ |
| **SURRENDERING Your Life for God's Pleasure** | |
| I am experiencing more of the presence and power of God in my everyday life. | 1 2 3 4 5 |
| I am faithfully attending services and my small group to worship God. | 1 2 3 4 5 |
| I am seeking to please God by surrendering every area of my life (health, decisions, finances, relationships, future, etc.) to him. | 1 2 3 4 5 |
| I am accepting the things I cannot change and becoming increasingly grateful for the life I've been given. | 1 2 3 4 5 |
| SURRENDERING Total | _____ |

Personal Health Assessment

| | Connecting | Growing | Serving | Sharing | Surrendering | |
|---|---|---|---|---|---|---|
| 20 | | | | | | Well Developed |
| 16 | | | | | | Very Good |
| 12 | | | | | | Getting Going |
| 8 | | | | | | Fair |
| 4 | | | | | | Just Beginning |

○ Beginning Assessment Total ________
□ Ending Assessment Total ________

# PERSONAL HEALTH PLAN

This worksheet could become your single most important feature in this study. On it you can record your personal priorities before the Father. It will help you live a healthy spiritual life, balancing all five of God's purposes.

| PURPOSE | PLAN |
|---|---|
| CONNECT | WHO are you connecting with spiritually? |
| GROW | WHAT is your next step for growth? |
| DEVELOP | WHERE are you serving? |
| SHARE | WHEN are you shepherding another in Christ? |
| SURRENDER | HOW are you surrendering your heart to God? |

| DATE | MY PROGRESS | PARTNER'S PROGRESS |
|---|---|---|
| | | |
| | | |
| | | |
| | | |
| | | |
| | | |

| DATE | MY PROGRESS | PARTNER'S PROGRESS |
|---|---|---|
| | | |
| | | |
| | | |
| | | |
| | | |
| | | |
| | | |
| | | |
| | | |
| | | |
| | | |
| | | |
| | | |
| | | |
| | | |
| | | |
| | | |
| | | |
| | | |

# SAMPLE PERSONAL HEALTH PLAN

This worksheet could become your single most important feature in this study. On it you can record your personal priorities before the Father. It will help you live a healthy spiritual life, balancing all five of God's purposes.

| PURPOSE | PLAN |
|---|---|
| CONNECT | WHO are you connecting with spiritually?<br>Bill and I will meet weekly by e-mail or phone |
| GROW | WHAT is your next step for growth?<br>Regular devotions or journaling my prayers 2×/week |
| DEVELOP | WHERE are you serving?<br>Serving in children's ministry<br>Go through GIFTS Assessment |
| SHARE | WHEN are you shepherding another in Christ?<br>Shepherding Bill at lunch or hosting a starter group in the fall |
| SURRENDER | HOW are you surrendering your heart?<br>Help with our teenager<br>New job situation |

Sample Personal Health Plan

| DATE | MY PROGRESS | PARTNER'S PROGRESS |
|---|---|---|
| 3/5 | Talked during our group | Figured out our goals together |
| 3/12 | Missed our time together | Missed our time together |
| 3/26 | Met for coffee and review of my goals | Met for coffee |
| 4/10 | E-mailed prayer requests | Bill sent me his prayer requests |
| 5/5 | Great start on personal journaling | Read Mark 1–6 in one sitting! |
| 5/12 | Traveled and not doing well this week | Journaled about Christ as healer |
| 5/26 | Back on track | Busy and distracted; asked for prayer |
| 6/1 | Need to call Children's Pastor | |
| 6/26 | Group did a serving project together | Agreed to lead group worship |
| 6/30 | Regularly rotating leadership | Led group worship–great job! |
| | | |
| 7/5 | Called Jim to see if he's open to joining our group | Wanted to invite somebody, but didn't |
| 7/12 | Preparing to start a group in fall | |
| 7/30 | Group prayed for me | Told friend something I'm learning about Christ |
| 8/5 | Overwhelmed but encouraged | Scared to lead worship |
| 8/15 | Felt heard and more settled | Issue with wife |
| 8/30 | Read book on teens | Glad he took on his fear |
| | | |
| | | |
| | | |
| | | |
| | | |
| | | |
| | | |
| | | |

# SPIRITUAL GIFTS INVENTORY

> A spiritual gift is given to each of us as a means of helping the entire church.
>
> 1 Corinthians 12:7 (NLT)

A spiritual gift is a special ability, given by the Holy Spirit to every believer at their conversion. Although spiritual gifts are given when the Holy Spirit enters new believers, their use and purpose need to be understood and developed as we grow spiritually. A spiritual gift is much like a muscle; the more you use it, the stronger it becomes.

**A Few Truths about Spiritual Gifts**

1. Only believers have spiritual gifts. 1 Corinthians 2:14
2. You can't earn or work for a spiritual gift. Ephesians 4:7
3. The Holy Spirit decides what gifts I get. 1 Corinthians 12:11
4. I am to develop the gifts God gives me. Romans 11:29; 2 Timothy 1:6
5. It's a sin to waste the gifts God gave me. 1 Corinthians 4:1–2; Matthew 25:14–30
6. Using my gifts honors God and expands me. John 15:8

## Gifts Inventory

God wants us to know what spiritual gift(s) he has given us. One person can have many gifts. The goal is to find the areas in which the Holy Spirit seems to have supernaturally empowered our service to others. These gifts are to be used to minister to others and build up the body of Christ.

There are four main lists of gifts found in the Bible in Romans 12:3–8; 1 Corinthians 12:1–11, 27–31; Ephesians 4:11–12; and 1 Peter 4:9–11. There are other passages that mention or illustrate gifts not included in these lists. As you read through this list, prayerfully consider whether the biblical definition describes you. Remember, you can have more than one gift, but everyone has at least one.

**ADMINISTRATION (Organization)—1 Corinthians 12**

This is the ability to recognize the gifts of others and recruit them to a ministry. It is the ability to organize and manage people, resources, and time for effective ministry.

**APOSTLE—1 Corinthians 12**

This is the ability to start new churches/ventures and oversee their development.

**DISCERNMENT—1 Corinthians 12**

This is the ability to distinguish between the spirit of truth and the spirit of error; to detect inconsistencies in another's life and confront in love.

**ENCOURAGEMENT (Exhortation)—Romans 12**

This is the ability to motivate God's people to apply and act on biblical principles, especially when they are discouraged or wavering in their faith. It is also the ability to bring out the best in others and challenge them to develop their potential.

**EVANGELISM—Ephesians 4**

This is the ability to communicate the gospel of Jesus Christ to unbelievers in a positive, nonthreatening way and to sense opportunities to share Christ and lead people to respond with faith.

**FAITH—1 Corinthians 12**

This is the ability to trust God for what cannot be seen and to act on God's promise, regardless of what the circumstances indicate. This includes a willingness to risk failure in pursuit of a God-given vision, expecting God to handle the obstacles.

**GIVING—Romans 12**

This is the ability to generously contribute material resources and/or money beyond the 10 percent tithe so that the church may grow and be strengthened. It includes the ability to manage money so it may be given to support the ministry of others.

**HOSPITALITY—1 Peter 4:9–10**

This is the ability to make others, especially strangers, feel warmly welcomed, accepted, and comfortable in the church family and the ability to coordinate factors that promote fellowship.

**LEADERSHIP—Romans 12**

This is the ability to clarify and communicate the purpose and direction ("vision") of a ministry in a way that attracts others to get involved, including the ability to motivate others, by example, to work together in accomplishing a ministry goal.

**MERCY—Romans 12**

This is the ability to manifest practical, compassionate, cheerful love toward suffering members of the body of Christ.

**PASTORING (Shepherding)—Ephesians 4**

This is the ability to care for the spiritual needs of a group of believers and equip them for ministry. It is also the ability to nurture a small group in spiritual growth and assume responsibility for their welfare.

**PREACHING—Romans 12**

This is the ability to publicly communicate God's Word in an inspired way that convinces unbelievers and both challenges and comforts believers.

**SERVICE—Romans 12**

This is the ability to recognize unmet needs in the church family, and take the initiative to provide practical assistance quickly, cheerfully, and without a need for recognition.

**TEACHING—Ephesians 4**

This is the ability to educate God's people by clearly explaining and applying the Bible in a way that causes them to learn; it is the ability to equip and train other believers for ministry.

**WISDOM—1 Corinthians 12**

This is the ability to understand God's perspective on life situations and share those insights in a simple, understandable way.

# TELLING YOUR STORY

First, don't underestimate the power of your testimony. Revelation 12:11 says, "They have defeated [Satan] by the blood of the Lamb and by their testimony. And they did not love their lives so much that they were afraid to die" (NLT).

A simple three-point approach is very effective in communicating your personal testimony. The approach focuses on before you trusted Christ, how you surrendered to him, and the difference in you since you've been walking with him. If you became a Christian at a very young age and don't remember what life was like before Christ, reflect on what you have seen in the lives of others. Before you begin, pray and ask God to give you the right words.

## Before You Knew Christ

Simply tell what your life was like before you surrendered to Christ. What was the key problem, emotion, situation, or attitude you were dealing with? What motivated you? What were your actions? How did you try to satisfy your inner needs? Create an interesting picture of your preconversion life and problems, and then explain what created a need and interest in Christian things.

## How You Came to Know Christ

How were you converted? Simply tell the events and circumstances that caused you to consider Christ as the solution to your needs. Take time to identify the steps that brought you to the point of trusting Christ. Where were you? What was happening at the time? What people or problems influenced your decision?

### The Difference Christ Has Made in Your Life

What is different about your life in Christ? How has his forgiveness impacted you? How have your thoughts, attitudes, and emotions changed? What problems have been resolved or changed? Share how Christ is meeting your needs and what a relationship with him means to you now. This should be the largest part of your story.

### Tips

- Don't use jargon: don't sound churchy, preachy, or pious.
- Stick to the point. Your conversion and new life in Christ should be the main points.
- Be specific. Include events, genuine feelings, and personal insights, both before and after conversion, which people would be interested in and that clarify your main point. This makes your testimony easier to relate to. Assume you are sharing with someone with no knowledge of the Christian faith.
- Be current. Tell what is happening in your life with God now, today.
- Be honest. Don't exaggerate or portray yourself as living a perfect life with no problems. This is not realistic. The simple truth of what God has done in your life is all the Holy Spirit needs to convict someone of their sin and convince them of his love and grace.
- Remember, it's the Holy Spirit who convicts. You need only be obedient and tell your story.
- When people reply to your efforts to share with statements like "I don't believe in God," "I don't believe the Bible is God's Word," or "How can a loving God allow suffering?" how can we respond to these replies?

- Above all, keep a positive attitude. Don't be defensive.
- Be sincere. This will speak volumes about your confidence in your faith.
- Don't be offended. It's not you they are rejecting.
- Pray—silently on-the-spot. Don't proceed without asking for God's help about the specific question. Seek his guidance on how, or if, you should proceed at this time.
- In God's wisdom, choose to do one of the following:
  - Postpone sharing at this time.
  - Answer their objections, if you can.
  - Promise to research their questions and return answers later.

**Step 1.** Everywhere Jesus went he used stories, or parables, to demonstrate our need for salvation. Through these stories, he helped people see the error of their ways, leading them to turn to him. Your story can be just as powerful today. Begin to develop your story by sharing what your life was like before you knew Christ. (If you haven't yet committed your life to Christ, or became a Christian at a very young age and don't remember what life was like before Christ, reflect on what you have seen in the life of someone close to you.) Make notes about this aspect of your story below and commit to writing it out this week.

____________________________________________

____________________________________________

____________________________________________

**Step 2.** Sit in groups of two or three people for this discussion. Review the "How You Came to Know Christ" section. Begin to develop this part of your story by sharing within your circle. Make notes about this aspect of your story below and commit to writing it out this week.

____________________________________________

____________________________________________

____________________________________________

**Step 2b.** Connecting: Go around the group and share about a time you were stopped cold while sharing Christ, by a question you couldn't answer. What happened?

**Step 2c.** Sharing: Previously we talked about the questions and objections we receive that stop us from continuing to share our faith with someone. These questions/objections might include:

- "I don't believe in God."
- "I don't believe the Bible is God's Word."
- "How can a loving God allow suffering?"

How can we respond to these replies?

**Step 3.** Subgroup into groups of two or three people for this discussion. Review "The Difference Christ Has Made in Your Life" section. Share the highlights of this part of your story within your circle. Make notes about this aspect of your story below and commit to writing it out this week.

____________________________________________

____________________________________________

____________________________________________

**Step 3b.** Story: There's nothing more exciting than a brand-new believer. My wife became a Christian four years before I met her. She was a flight attendant at the time. Her zeal to introduce others to Jesus was reminiscent of the woman at the well who ran and got the whole town out to see Jesus.

My wife immediately began an international organization of Christian flight attendants for fellowship and for reaching out to others in their profession. She organized events where many people came to Christ, and bid for trips with another flight attendant who was a Christian so they could witness on the planes. They even bid for the shorter trips so they could talk to as many different people as possible. They had a goal for every flight to talk to at least one person about Christ, and to be encouraged by at least one person who already knew him. God met that request every time.

In her zeal, however, she went home to her family over the holidays and vacations and had little or no success. Later she would realize that she pressed them too hard. Jesus said a prophet is without honor in his own town, and I think the same goes for family. That's because members of your family think they know you, and are more likely to ignore changes, choosing instead to see you as they've always seen you. "Isn't this the carpenter's son—the son of Joseph?" they said of Jesus. "Don't we know this guy?"

With family members you have to walk with Christ openly and be patient. Change takes time. And remember, we don't save anyone. We just introduce them to Jesus through telling our own story. God does the rest.

**Step 4.** As a group, review *Telling Your Story*. Share which part of your story is the most difficult for you to tell. Which is the easiest for you? If you have time, a few of you share your story with the group.

**Step 5.** Throughout this study we have had the opportunity to develop our individual testimonies. One way your group can serve each other is to provide a safe forum for "practicing" telling your stories. Continue to take turns sharing your testimonies now. Set a time limit—say two to three minutes each. Don't miss this great opportunity to get to know one another better and encourage each other's growth too.

# SERVING COMMUNION

Churches vary in their treatment of communion (or the Lord's Supper). We offer one simple form by which a small group can share this experience together. You can adapt this as necessary, or omit it from your group altogether, depending on your church's beliefs.

**Steps in Serving Communion**

1. Open by sharing about God's love, forgiveness, grace, mercy, commitment, tenderheartedness, faithfulness, etc., out of your personal journey (connect with the stories of those in the room).
2. Read one or several of the passages listed below.
3. Pray and pass the bread around the circle.
4. When everyone has been served, remind them that this represents Jesus's broken body on their behalf. Simply state, "Jesus said, 'Do this in remembrance of me' (Luke 22:19 NIV). Let us eat together," and eat the bread as a group.
5. Then read the rest of the passage: "In the same way, after the supper he took the cup, saying, 'This cup is the new covenant in my blood, which is poured out for you'" (Luke 22:20 NIV).
6. Pray, and serve the cups, either by passing a small tray, serving them individually, or having members pick up a cup from the table.
7. When everyone has been served, remind them the juice represents Christ's blood shed for them, then simply state, "Take and drink in remembrance of him. Let us drink together."
8. Finish by singing a simple song, listening to a praise song, or having a time of prayer in thanks to God.

Communion passages: Matthew 26:26–29; Mark 14:22–25; Luke 22:14–20; 1 Corinthians 10:16–21; 11:17–34.

# PERFORMING A FOOTWASHING

*Scripture:* John 13:1–17. Jesus makes it quite clear to his disciples that his position as the Father's Son includes being a servant rather than power and glory only. To properly understand the scene and the intention of Jesus, we must realize that the washing of feet was the duty of slaves and indeed of non-Jewish rather than Jewish slaves. Jesus placed himself in the position of a servant. He displayed to the disciples self-sacrifice and love. In view of his majesty, only the symbolic position of a slave was adequate to open their eyes and keep them from lofty illusions. The point of footwashing, then, is to correct the attitude that Jesus discerned in the disciples. It constitutes the permanent basis for mutual service, service in your group and for the community around you, which is the responsibility of all Christians.

## When to Implement

There are three primary places we would recommend you insert a footwashing: during a break in the Surrendering section of your group; during a break in the Growing section of your group; or at the closing of your group. A special time of prayer for each person as he or she gets his or her feet washed can be added to the footwashing time.

# SURRENDERING AT THE CROSS

Surrendering everything to God is one of the most challenging aspects of following Jesus. It involves a relationship built on trust and faith. Each of us is in a different place on our spiritual journey. Some of us have known the Lord for many years, some are new in our faith, and some may still be checking God out. Regardless, we all have things that we still want control over—things we don't want to give to God because we don't know what he will do with them. These things are truly more important to us than God is—they have become our god.

We need to understand that God wants us to be completely devoted to him. If we truly love God with all our heart, soul, strength, and mind (Luke 10:27), we will be willing to give him everything.

**Steps in Surrendering at the Cross**

1. You will need some small pieces of paper and pens or pencils for people to write down the things they want to sacrifice/surrender to God.
2. If you have a wooden cross, hammers, and nails you can have the members nail their sacrifices to the cross. If you don't have a wooden cross, get creative. Think of another way to symbolically relinquish the sacrifices to God. You might use a fireplace to burn them in the fire as an offering to the Lord. The point is giving to the Lord whatever hinders your relationship with him.

3. Create an atmosphere conducive to quiet reflection and prayer. Whatever this quiet atmosphere looks like for your group, do the best you can to create a peaceful time to meet with God.
4. Once you are settled, prayerfully think about the points below. Let the words and thoughts draw you into a heart-to-heart connection with your Lord Jesus Christ.

   - ☐ ***Worship him.*** Ask God to change your viewpoint so you can worship him through a surrendered spirit.
   - ☐ ***Humble yourself.*** Surrender doesn't happen without humility. James 4:6–7 says: "'God opposes the proud but gives grace to the humble.' Submit yourselves, then, to God" (NIV).
   - ☐ ***Surrender your mind, will, and emotions.*** This is often the toughest part of surrendering. What do you sense God urging you to give him so you can have the kind of intimacy he desires with you? Our hearts yearn for this kind of connection with him; let go of the things that stand between you.
   - ☐ ***Write out your prayer.*** Write out your prayer of sacrifice and surrender to the Lord. This may be an attitude, a fear, a person, a job, a possession—anything that God reveals is a hindrance to your relationship with him.

5. After writing out your sacrifice, take it to the cross and offer it to the Lord. Nail your sacrifice to the cross, or burn it as a sacrifice in the fire.
6. Close by singing, praying together, or taking communion. Make this time as short or as long as seems appropriate for your group.

Surrendering to God is life-changing and liberating. God desires that we be overcomers! First John 4:4 says, "You, dear children, are from God and have overcome . . . because the one who is in you is greater than the one who is in the world" (NIV).

# JOURNALING 101

Henri Nouwen says effective and lasting ministry *for* God grows out of a quiet place alone *with* God. This is why journaling is so important.

The greatest adventure of our lives is found in the daily pursuit of knowing, growing in, serving, sharing, and worshiping Christ forever. This is the essence of a purposeful life: to see all these biblical purposes fully formed and balanced in our lives. Only then are we "complete in Christ" (Col. 1:28 NASB).

David poured his heart out to God by writing psalms. The book of Psalms contains many of his honest conversations with God in written form, including expressions of every imaginable emotion on every aspect of his life. Like David, we encourage you to select a strategy to integrate God's Word and journaling into your devotional time. Use any of the following resources:

- Bible
- Bible reading plan
- Devotional
- Topical Bible study plan

Before and after you read a portion of God's Word, speak to God in honest reflection in the form of a written prayer. You may begin this time by simply finishing the sentence "Father, . . . ," "Yesterday, Lord, . . . ," or "Thank you, God, for, . . . ." Share with him where you are at the present moment; express your hurts, disappointments, frustrations, blessings, victories, and gratefulness. Whatever you do with your journal, make a plan that fits you, so you'll have a positive experience. Consider sharing highlights of your progress and experiences with some or all of your group members, especially your spiritual partner. You may find they want to join and even encourage you in this journey. Most of all, enjoy the ride and cultivate a more authentic, growing walk with God.

# PRAYER AND PRAISE REPORT

Briefly share your prayer requests with the large group, making notations below. Then gather in small groups of two to four to pray for each other.

Date: ________________

Prayer Requests

________________________________________

________________________________________

________________________________________

________________________________________

________________________________________

Praise Reports

________________________________________

________________________________________

________________________________________

________________________________________

________________________________________

## Prayer and Praise Report

Briefly share your prayer requests with the large group, making notations below. Then gather in small groups of two to four to pray for each other.

Date: ________________

Prayer Requests

____________________________________________________________

____________________________________________________________

____________________________________________________________

____________________________________________________________

____________________________________________________________

Praise Reports

____________________________________________________________

____________________________________________________________

____________________________________________________________

____________________________________________________________

____________________________________________________________

## Prayer and Praise Report

Briefly share your prayer requests with the large group, making notations below. Then gather in small groups of two to four to pray for each other.

Date: ________________

Prayer Requests

____________________________________________________________

____________________________________________________________

____________________________________________________________

____________________________________________

____________________________________________

Praise Reports

____________________________________________

____________________________________________

____________________________________________

____________________________________________

____________________________________________

## Prayer and Praise Report

Briefly share your prayer requests with the large group, making notations below. Then gather in small groups of two to four to pray for each other.

Date: ________________

Prayer Requests

____________________________________________

____________________________________________

____________________________________________

____________________________________________

____________________________________________

Praise Reports

____________________________________________

____________________________________________

____________________________________________

____________________________________________

____________________________________________

## Prayer and Praise Report

Briefly share your prayer requests with the large group, making notations below. Then gather in small groups of two to four to pray for each other.

Date: ________________

Prayer Requests

________________________________________

________________________________________

________________________________________

________________________________________

________________________________________

Praise Reports

________________________________________

________________________________________

________________________________________

________________________________________

________________________________________

# SMALL GROUP ROSTER

| Name | Address | Phone | E-mail Address | Team or Role | When/How to Contact You |
|---|---|---|---|---|---|
| Bill Jones | 7 Alvalar Street L.F. 92665 | 766-2255 | bjones@aol.com | Socials | Evenings After 5 |
| | | | | | |
| | | | | | |
| | | | | | |
| | | | | | |
| | | | | | |
| | | | | | |
| | | | | | |
| | | | | | |

(Pass your book around your group at your first meeting to get everyone's name and contact information.)

| Name | Address | Phone | E-mail Address | Team or Role | When/How to Contact You |
|---|---|---|---|---|---|
| | | | | | |
| | | | | | |
| | | | | | |
| | | | | | |
| | | | | | |
| | | | | | |
| | | | | | |
| | | | | | |
| | | | | | |

# LEADING FOR THE FIRST TIME

## *LEADERSHIP 101*

**Sweaty palms are a healthy sign.** The Bible says God is gracious to the humble. Remember who is in control; the time to worry is when you're not worried. Those who are soft in heart (and sweaty-palmed) are those whom God is sure to speak through.

**Seek support.** Ask your leader, coleader, or close friend to pray for you and prepare with you before the session. Walking through the study will help you anticipate potentially difficult questions and discussion topics.

**Bring your uniqueness to the study.** Lean into who you are and how God wants you to uniquely lead the study.

**Prepare. Prepare. Prepare.** Go through the session several times. If you are using the DVD, listen to the teaching segment and *Leader Lifter*. Consider writing in a journal or fasting for a day to prepare yourself for what God wants to do.

**Don't wait until the last minute to prepare.**

**Ask for feedback so you can grow.** Perhaps in an e-mail or on cards handed out at the study, have everyone write down three things you did well and one thing you could improve on. Don't get defensive, but show an openness to learn and grow.

**Prayerfully consider launching a new group.** This doesn't need to happen overnight, but God's heart is for this to happen over time. Not all Christians are called to be leaders or teachers, but we are all called to be "shepherds" of a few someday.

**Share with your group what God is doing in your heart.** God is searching for those whose hearts are fully his. Share your trials and victories. We promise that people will relate.

**Prayerfully consider whom you would like to pass the baton to next week.** It's only fair. God is ready for the next member of your group to go on the faith journey you just traveled. Make it fun, and expect God to do the rest.

# LEADER'S NOTES

## *INTRODUCTION*

Congratulations! You have responded to the call to help shepherd Jesus's flock. There are few other tasks in the family of God that surpass the contribution you will be making. We have provided you several ways to prepare for this role. Between the *Read Me First*, these *Leader's Notes*, and the *Watch This First* and *Leader Lifter* segments on the optional *Deepening Life Together: John* Video Teaching DVD, you'll have all you need to do a great job of leading your group. Just don't forget, you are not alone. God knew that you would be asked to lead this group and he won't let you down. In Hebrews 13:5b God promises us, "Never will I leave you; never will I forsake you" (NIV).

Your role as leader is to create a safe, warm environment for your group. As a leader, your most important job is to create an atmosphere where people are willing to talk honestly about what the topics discussed in this study have to do with them. Be available before people arrive so you can greet them at the door. People are naturally nervous at a new group, so a hug or handshake can help put them at ease. Before you start leading your group, a little preparation will give you confidence. Review the *Read Me First* at the front of your study guide so you'll understand the purpose of each section, enabling you to help your group understand it as well.

If you're new to leading a group, congratulations and thank you; this will be a life-changing experience for you also. We have provided these *Leader's Notes* to help new leaders begin well.

It's important in your first meeting to make sure group members understand that things shared personally and in prayer must remain confidential. Also, be careful not to dominate the group discussion, but facilitate it and encourage others to join in and share. And lastly, have fun.

Take a moment at the beginning of your first meeting to orient the group to one principle that undergirds this study: A healthy small group balances the purposes of the church. Most small groups emphasize Bible study, fellowship, and prayer. But God has called us to reach out to others as well. He wants us to do what Jesus teaches, not just learn about it.

**Preparing for each meeting ahead of time.** Take the time to review the session, the *Leader's Notes*, and *Leader Lifter* for the session before each session. Also write down your answers to each question. Pay special attention to exercises that ask group members to *do* something. These exercises will help your group live out what the Bible teaches, not just talk about it. Be sure you understand how the exercises work, and bring any supplies you might need, such as paper or pens. Pray for your group members by name at least once between sessions and before each session. Use the *Prayer and Praise Report* so you will remember their prayer requests. Ask God to use your time together to touch the heart of every person. Expect God to give you the opportunity to talk with those he wants you to encourage or challenge in a special way.

**Don't try to go it alone.** Pray for God to help you. Ask other members of your group to help by taking on some small role. In the *Appendix* you'll find the *Team Roles* pages with some suggestions to get people involved. Leading is more rewarding if you give group members opportunities to help. Besides, helping group members discover their individual gifts for serving or even leading the group will bless all of you.

Consider asking a few people to come early to help set up, pray, and introduce newcomers to others. Even if everyone is new, they don't know that yet and may be shy when they arrive. You might give people roles like setting up name tags or handing out drinks. This could be a great way to spot a co-leader.

**Subgrouping.** If your group has more than seven people, break into discussion groups of three to four people for the *Growing* and *Surrendering* sections each week. People will connect more with the study and each other when they have more opportunity to participate. Smaller discussion circles encourage quieter people to talk more and tend to minimize the effects of more vocal or dominant members. Also, people who are unaccustomed to praying aloud will feel more comfortable praying within a smaller group of people. Share prayer requests in the larger group and then break into smaller groups to pray for each other. People are more willing to pray in small circles if they know that the whole group will hear all the prayer requests.

**Memorizing Scripture.** At the start of each session you will find a memory verse—a verse for the group to memorize each week. Encourage your group members to do this. Memorizing God's Word is both directed and celebrated throughout the Bible, either explicitly ("Your word I have hidden in my heart, that I might not sin against You" [Ps. 119:11 NKJV]), or implicitly, as in the example of our Lord ("He departed to the mountain to pray" [Mark 6:46 NKJV]).

Anyone who has memorized Scripture can confirm the amazing spiritual benefits that result from this practice. Don't miss out on the opportunity to encourage your group to grow in the knowledge of God's Word through Scripture memorization.

**Reflections.** We've provided opportunity for a personal time with God using the *Reflections* at the end of each session. Don't press seekers to do this, but just remind the group that every believer should have a plan for personal time with God.

**Inviting new people.** Cast the vision, as Jesus did, to be inclusive not exclusive. Ask everyone to prayerfully think of people who would enjoy or benefit from a group like this—then invite them. The beginning of a new study is a great time to welcome a few people into your circle. Don't worry about ending up with too many people—you can always have one discussion circle in the living room and another in the dining room.

**For Deeper Study (Optional).** We have included a *For Deeper Study* section in each session. *For Deeper Study* provides additional passages for individual study on the topic of each session. If your group likes to do deeper Bible study, consider having members study the *For Deeper Study* passages for homework. Then, during the *Growing* portion of your meeting, you can share the high points of what you've learned.

# LEADER'S NOTES
## *SESSIONS*

### Session One The Prologue of John

*Connecting*

1. We've designed this study for both new and established groups, and for both seekers and the spiritually mature. New groups will need to invest more time building relationships with each other. Established groups often want to dig deeper into Bible study and application. Regardless of whether your group is new or has been together for a while, be sure to answer this introductory question at this first session.

2. A very important item in this first session is the *Small Group Agreement.* An agreement helps clarify your group's priorities and cast new vision for what the group can become. You can find this in the *Appendix* of this study guide. We've found that groups that talk about these values up front and commit to an agreement benefit significantly. They work through conflicts long before people get to the point of frustration, so there's a lot less pain.

   Take some time to review this agreement before your meeting. Then during your meeting, read the agreement aloud to the entire group. If some people have concerns about a specific item or the agreement as a whole, be sensitive to their concerns. Explain that tens of thousands of groups use agreements like this one as a simple tool for building trust and group health over time.

   We recommend talking about shared ownership of the group. It's important that each member have a role. See the *Appendix* to learn more about Team Roles. This is a great tool to get this important practice launched in your group.

*Growing*

Have someone read Bible passages aloud. It's a good idea to ask ahead of time, because not everyone is comfortable reading aloud in public.

4. The Word already existed at the beginning of the universe. The Word was with God, yet the Word was God. (Passages like this lead us to understand God as a Trinity, three persons in one God.) Verses 3–5 tell us that through the Word all things were made; nothing was made without him. Life was in him, and the Word's life is the light of people. He is the light in many ways. For instance, in the sense of pure goodness, pure truth—illumination for those who are confused, goodness that triumphs over evil. John calls him "the Word" for many reasons. For instance, the Word reveals God the way a person's words express who he is. Also, when God speaks, powerful things happen. The Word is powerful, active.

5. Both verses speak of the beginning and creation. Genesis says in the beginning God created . . . , whereas John 1:1 says in the beginning was. . . . The conclusion is that the Word existed even before God created our physical universe.

6. In 1:14 John applies human attributes to the Word. He applies personal pronouns to the Word and says, "the Word became flesh and made his dwelling (or lived) among us." This "becoming flesh" tells us that the Word is Jesus Christ, God in human flesh. Jesus was personally involved in the creation of our universe. He is also the source of spiritual enlightenment, and real life is found in him.

7. John came as a witness to confirm that the light (the Messiah) had come and what that meant to humanity. As Christ's followers, it is important that we confirm to the world around us that Jesus is the way to true life.

8. Jesus came first to those of his own lineage, the Jews, and they didn't receive him.

9. Although most of Jesus's fellow Jews rejected him, some believed. And some non-Jews believed. All of these, Jews and non-Jews, who received him (believed in his name) were given the right to become children of God. That offer of rebirth as God's child remains for people today. To be born of God is to come alive spiritually with a new family identity (God's family) and new "DNA" guiding who we will grow up to be.

10. The Word, Jesus, revealed his glory to humanity by descending into the world as a flesh-and-blood human being. As Christ lived among his disciples, he displayed attributes of God such as grace, mercy, wisdom, righteousness, truth, etc. These attributes reveal God's unfailing love and faithfulness to humanity. The divine Word's willingness to humble himself to take on human flesh shows God's passionate, no-holds-barred love for humans.

11. Through Jesus's humanity we are able to see and understand God. Jesus is not merely a human reflection of God; he is God and therefore gives humanity the exact and authentic representation of God's character. He

knows what it's like to be a man and live in a fallen world. He has been here where we are. And when we read about how Jesus talked and behaved, we see God in action.

12. Deuteronomy 32:46–47 tells us that the law is life; apart from keeping the law and the sacrifices, there is no hope of being in a right relationship with God.

13. The law revealed God's demand for holiness. This showed humankind our unrighteousness and therefore illuminated our need for a Savior. Jesus came as a demonstration of God's grace (his undeserved favor despite our failure to obey him) and truth (his reliability as the standard of what is accurate and real). The Law can't change us, but grace and truth can forgive us, restore relationship, and transform us.

*Developing*

This section enables you to help the group see the importance of developing their abilities for service to God.

15. The intent of this question is to encourage group members to set aside some time to spend with God in prayer and his Word at home each day throughout the week. Read through this section and be prepared to help the group understand how important it is to fill our minds with the Word of God. If people already have a good Bible reading plan and commitment, that is great, but you may have people who struggle to stay in the Word daily. Sometimes beginning with a simple commitment to a short daily reading can start a habit that changes their life.

    The *Reflections* pages at the end of each session include verses that were either talked about in the session or support the teaching of the session. They are very short readings with a few lines to encourage people to write down their thoughts. Remind the group about these *Reflections* each week after the *Surrendering* section. Encourage the group to commit to a next step in prayer, Bible reading, or meditation on the Word.

*Sharing*

Jesus wants all of his disciples to help outsiders connect with him, to know him personally. This section should provide an opportunity to go beyond Bible study to biblical living.

16. This activity should get the group to observe their interactions during the coming week with the intention of using these observations next week in evaluating the people whom God has placed in their lives that he might want them to share with or invite to small group.

*Surrendering*

God is most pleased by a heart that is fully his. Each group session will provide group members a chance to surrender their hearts to God in prayer and worship. Group prayer requests and prayer time should be included every week.

17. Encourage group members to use the *Reflections* verses in their daily quiet time throughout the week. This will move them closer to God while reinforcing the lesson of this session through related Scripture.
18. As you move to a time of sharing prayer requests, be sure to remind the group of the importance of confidentiality and keeping what is shared in the group within the group. Everyone must feel that the personal things they share will be kept in confidence if you are to have safety and bonding within the group members.

*For Deeper Study*

We have included an optional *For Deeper Study* section in each session. *For Deeper Study* provides additional passages for individual study on the topic of each session. If your group likes to do deeper Bible study, consider having members study the *For Deeper Study* passages at home between meetings.

**Session Two First Sign from the Messiah**

*Connecting*

2. We encourage the group to rotate leaders and hosts homes each meeting. This practice will go a long way toward bonding the group. Review the *Small Group Calendar* and talk about who else is willing to open their home or facilitate a meeting. Rotating host homes and leadership along with implementing *Team Roles* as discussed in *Session One* will quickly move the group ownership from "your group" to "our group."

*Growing*

4. John denies that he is the Christ, saying he is the voice of one calling in the wilderness, preparing the way for the Lord. In Isaiah 40:3, Isaiah hears a voice calling Israel to prepare for the Lord's coming. The Lord is coming to free Israel from captivity in Babylon. Yet centuries later when John comes, the Jews are still under foreign domination, waiting for a Messiah who will free them. John humbly refers to himself as the voice who calls,

the forerunner who prepares the people for the coming Messiah (or who calls the people to prepare).

5. "Lamb of God" would have come as a surprise to John's followers, because at that time no one knew that the Messiah would be killed like the animals sacrificed in the temple. But John somehow knew and pointed to Jesus's sacrificial role. The Jews were looking for a Messiah to be a military leader; John pointed to a quite different kind of Messiah. Seeing the Spirit descend on Jesus was the signal to John that God had sent his promised Messiah. It was the signal for John's ministry to begin fading out as Jesus's took off (see chapter 3).

6. Jesus doesn't hesitate to invite John's disciples to switch and become his disciples. He knows who he is. He also knows that John won't see this as stealing disciples. Group members may have different responses, but many may notice how Jesus invites these young men to "come and see" who he is. This is an invitation to relationship. Also, Jesus is a bit enigmatic.

7. Jesus knows more than an ordinary person would know, and he uses his insight to gently draw Nathanael to become curious and inquire further. Instead of demanding allegiance, Jesus invites and intrigues. Jesus promises Nathanael will see greater things, including confirmation by the Spirit of who Jesus is. Jesus compares himself to a ladder by which angels might ascend and descend to and from heaven. Jesus is the link between earth and heaven.

8. This is the first of eight miracles recorded in the Gospel of John that confirm who Jesus is.

9. Jesus signifies his role in inaugurating the new age of salvation and the "messianic banquet," an Old Testament picture of God's final salvation (Isa. 25:6–8).

10. The group will have various ideas about what brings people to true faith in Christ today. They may consider things like seeing changes in us after we come to Christ, the testimony of the Bible, the witness of the Holy Spirit in their hearts and minds. Be open to different points of view. With this type of question, there are many right answers, and the point is to share ideas.

*Developing*

11. For many, spiritual partners will be a new idea. We highly encourage you to try pairs for this study. It's so hard to start a spiritual practice like prayer or consistent Bible reading with no support. A friend makes a huge difference. As leader, you may want to prayerfully decide who would be a good match with whom. Remind people that this partnership isn't forever; it's just for a

few weeks. Be sure to have extra copies of the *Personal Health Plan* available at this meeting in case you need to have a group of three spiritual partners. It is a good idea for you to look over the *Personal Health Plan* before the meeting so you can help people understand how to use it.

Instruct your group members to enlist a spiritual partner by asking them to pair up with someone in the group (we suggest that men partner with men and women with women) and turn to the *Personal Health Plan*.

Ask the group to complete the instructions for the WHO and WHAT questions on the *Personal Health Plan*. Your group has now begun to address two of God's purposes for their lives!

You can see that the *Personal Health Plan* contains space to record the ups and downs and progress each week in the column labeled "My Progress." When partners check in each week, they can record their partner's progress in the goal he or she chose in the "Partner's Progress" column on this chart. You'll find a *Sample Personal Health Plan* filled in as an example.

### *Sharing*

13. A *Circles of Life* diagram is provided for you and the group to use to help you identify people who need a connection to Christian community. Encourage the group to commit to praying for God's guidance and an opportunity to reach out to each person in their *Circles of Life*.

    We encourage this outward focus for your group because groups that become too inwardly focused tend to become unhealthy over time. People naturally gravitate toward feeding themselves through Bible study, prayer, and social time, so it's usually up to the leader to push them to consider how this inward nourishment can overflow into outward concern for others. Never forget: Jesus came to seek and save the lost and to find a shepherd for every sheep.

    Talk to the group about the importance of inviting people; remind them that healthy small groups make a habit of inviting friends, neighbors, unconnected church members, co-workers, etc., to join their groups or join them at a weekend service. When people get connected to a group of new friends, they often join the church.

    Some groups are happy with the people they already have in the group and they don't really want to grow larger. Some fear that newcomers will interrupt the intimacy that members have built over time. However, groups generally gain strength with the infusion of new people. It's like a river of living water flowing into a stagnant pond. Some groups remain permanently open, while others open periodically, such as at the beginning and ending of a study. If your circle becomes too large for easy face-to-face conversations, you can simply form a second or third discussion circle in another room in your home.

*Surrendering*

14. Be sure to remind the group of the importance of confidentiality and keeping what is shared in the group within the group. Use the *Prayer and Praise Report* in the *Appendix* to record your prayer requests.

15. Last week we talked briefly about incorporating *Reflections* into the group members' daily time with God. Some people don't yet have an established quiet time. With this in mind, engage a discussion with the group about the importance of making daily time with God a priority. Talk about potential obstacles and practical ideas for how to overcome them. The *Reflections* verses could serve as a springboard for drawing near to God. So don't forget these are a valuable resource for your group.

## Session Three Early Ministry in Jerusalem and Samaria

*Connecting*

1. Encourage group members to take time to complete the *Personal Health Assessment*. In the next question you will have the opportunity to pair up spiritual partners to discuss one thing that is going well and one thing that needs work. Participants should not be asked to share any aspect of this assessment in the large group if they don't want to.

*Growing*

4. Nicodemus, a member of the Jewish ruling council, comes to Jesus, recognizing him as one empowered by God. He probably comes at night because of the implications of openly associating with Jesus. Also, night suggests his darkened understanding at this point in his story (see 3:19–21).

5. In 3:3, rebirth suggests that Jesus is talking about a total renewal of who a person is, not just a little moral improvement here and there. The source of this new life and identity is the Spirit of God (3:8).

8. Jesus's mission is to save the world, not to condemn it. Yet people, by their own choices, may condemn themselves. The coming of him who is the Light gives everyone a choice: Come toward the light and receive more light; or flee from the light to hide your evil deeds, and be left in darkness. Over and over in John's Gospel, Jesus gives people this choice between light and darkness.

9. Jesus meets this Samaritan woman at a well and asks her for a drink. When she wonders why a respectable Jew like him would speak with her, a hated Samaritan and a woman, he offers her "living water." He continually piques her interest with cryptic statements and bewildering knowledge about her.

Just as our physical lives depend on physical water, eternal life for our thirsty souls requires the water that Jesus gives, salvation and the Holy Spirit.

11. Jesus has such an impact on this woman that she risks ridicule to tell as many people as she can about Jesus. Many Samaritans believed in him as a result. She is a model of a person who responds to Jesus in faith and is reborn, transformed.

*Developing*

14. Group members should consider where they can take a next step toward getting involved in ministering to the body of Christ in your local church. Discuss some of the ministries that your church may offer to people looking to get involved, such as the children's ministry, ushering, or hospitality. Remind everyone that it sometimes takes time and trying several different ministries before finding the one that fits best.

*Sharing*

16. It is important to return to the *Circles of Life* diagram and encourage the group to follow through on their commitments to invite people who need to know Christ more deeply through Christian community. When people are asked why they never go to church, they often say, "No one ever invited me." Remind the group that our responsibility is to invite people, but it is the Holy Spirit's responsibility to compel them to come.

## Session Four More Signs and Miracles from the Messiah

*Growing*

This session covers John 5–6. Reading the entire selection aloud may be time-consuming so it is recommended that you ask the group to read these passages at home before coming to the group.

4. These Jewish leaders are focused on enforcing the Old Testament law and the regulations based on rabbinic interpretations and oral traditions about the law. The law forbids work on the Sabbath, and the rabbis interpret carrying something like a mat as work. Healing someone is also work. These Bible scholars can't imagine that someone who violates their Bible interpretations could be sent from God.

5. Jesus claims things that only God could legitimately claim about himself. He refers to God as "my Father," an intimacy unheard of among Jews of his time. He says he submits to the Father's will, yet he is equal to the Father in his person (vv. 17, 18), his works (vv. 19–20), his power and sovereignty

(v. 21), his judgment (v. 22), and his honor (v. 23). He works as the Father works. He does what the Father does. He has the power to give life. He has the authority to judge. He has life in himself, not life from another source like ordinary men.

6. Just as Jesus provokes people in the story to respond to him in various ways, John's intent is that the reader decide how to respond to Jesus. If Jesus is who he claims to be here, then he deserves our absolute trust, regardless of the challenges we face in our lives. Not just theoretical belief but active trust. What would acting on complete trust in Jesus as the source of life look like in your life this week?

7. The people are thinking in very material terms. Jesus can do miracles like Moses, so he must be the military king they've been looking for, who will drive the Romans out of Israel. They like having their stomachs filled, but they still want Jesus to conform to their idea of a Messiah, and they're not interested in having their idea challenged.

9. He wants people to believe in him as one sent from the Father, as the Bread of Life. He wants people to come to him with total allegiance and commitment. He asks them to eat his flesh and drink his blood—an incredibly graphic image.

10. The crowd hearing these words the first time would have no idea what Jesus is talking about. Jesus is alluding to the blood sacrifice that he will eventually become. Jewish worshipers ate the flesh of sacrificed animals as if sharing a meal with God, but drinking blood was associated with pagan sacrifices to idols. Some say Jesus's words would have reminded John's original readers of the Lord's Supper, the bread and wine they shared to identify with Jesus in his self-sacrifice. Others say Jesus is simply talking about assimilating his revelation and wisdom into the deepest part of oneself, feeding on it spiritually in order to live and serve Christ in the world. If group members find Jesus's graphic words distressing, you might point out that many of his disciples had similar problems with the way he talked (6:60).

11. It's important for all of us to ask ourselves, "What do I treat as my food, the source of my life?" For some it's money, possessions, success, sex, romance, entertainment, religion, approval from others—there are countless possibilities. Just deciding to spend time every day feeding on Jesus's presence is a statement that he, not these other things, is the one who gives us life.

### *Developing*

12. This activity provides an opportunity for the group to share the love of Jesus by meeting real, felt needs. Discuss this with everyone and choose one action step to take as a group. Be certain that everyone understands his or

her role in this activity. It might be a good idea to call each person during the week to be sure they don't forget to bring to the next session what is required of them.

Designate one person to investigate where to donate items in your area. That person can also be responsible for dropping off the items.

13. Point the group to the *Spiritual Gifts Inventory* in the *Appendix*. Read through the spiritual gifts and engage the group in discussion about which gifts they believe they have. Encourage everyone to review these further on their own time during the coming week, giving prayerful consideration to each one.

*Sharing*

15. Encourage group members to consider developing their salvation story as a tool for sharing their faith with others. Begin the process during your group time and encourage the group to complete the exercise at home. As leader, you should review the "Tips" section of *Telling Your Story* yourself in advance and be ready to share your ideas about this process with the group.

**Session Five Jesus in Jerusalem for the Feasts of Tabernacles and Dedication**

*Growing*

This session covers chapters 7 and 8 only briefly, chapter 9 in more depth, and skips chapter 10. Please encourage group members to read chapters 7–10 at home before coming to the group, or afterward.

4. The Jews at this feast would be familiar with the Old Testament allusions Jesus is making. See Ezekiel 47:1–9 and Zechariah 13:1. Jesus's claims go way beyond what the Jews expected from a Messiah. They are claims only God could make.

   Some group members may be uncomfortable talking about their experience of the Holy Spirit. But here is a promise from Jesus about what should be normal for Christians. What does Jesus mean?

5. We've seen John use the imagery of light and darkness before. Jesus's hearers would have in mind passages like Isaiah 42:6–7 and Isaiah 62:19–22. Darkness indicates sin, evil, spiritual blindness. Following Jesus leads to more and more mental and moral enlightenment—to wisdom, knowledge of God, and goodness.

6. Jesus says this man's blindness was not caused by his own sin or his parents' sin, but the purpose was to reveal God's work. Jesus is not denying

that a connection exists between sin and suffering, but rejects the notion that personal sin is the direct cause of suffering in a case like this. God's sovereignty and unique plan for each individual play a part in the sufferings we endure.

7. At first the man's healing is purely physical, and he has no idea about who healed him. He just knows that a man put mud on his eyes, he washed and then he could see. In verse 17, he says the man must have been a prophet. By verses 30–38, the healed man is convinced that the one who healed him was a man from God or he would not have been able to open the eyes of someone who was born blind. He sticks to what he knows is true, despite pressure to back down, and so he comes to see more and more of the truth about Jesus. Eventually Jesus tells him who he is, and the man worships him. This story mirrors our understanding of God as we come to him with little knowledge and grow over time in understanding who he is and what we have in him spiritually.

8. They refuse to take into themselves the evidence that points to Jesus being from God, because they are wedded to their interpretation of the Bible's commands. Despite logic and evidence, they cling to their presuppositions, and are even willing to insult and persecute the healed man for standing by the truth. The blindness of those who claim they can already see is the one kind of blindness Jesus can't heal and forgive, because it is a blindness that rejects his help (9:41).

9. As Jesus himself said in John 9:3, the purpose of this sign, or miracle, is to demonstrate the powerful work of God in one's personal life and circumstances.

### *Developing*

14. Encourage group members to use the *Personal Health Plan* to jot down their next step to serving in ministry, with a plan for how and when they will begin.

### *Sharing*

15. This activity provides an opportunity for the group to share Jesus in a very practical way. Discuss this with everyone and choose one action step to take as a group. Be certain that everyone understands his or her role in this activity. It might be a good idea to call each person during the week to be sure they don't forget to bring to the next session what is required of them.

    Designate one person to investigate where to donate items in your area. That person can also be responsible for dropping off the items.

## Session Six Raising Lazarus and Coming to Jerusalem

*Growing*

3. Because God alone can raise the dead, Jesus waits until Lazarus is dead and buried before he helps him. "Glorify" is an important word in John's Gospel. God and his Son will be glorified through a sign that reveals Jesus's power and identity. They will also be glorified through the ultimate sign, Jesus's death and resurrection (12:23–28; 17:1–5).

   The blind man in John 9 and Lazarus in John 11 are unique cases in that God chooses them to play unique roles in revealing that Jesus is the Messiah. God chooses them to experience miracles that will reveal Jesus during his earthly ministry. Not every incident of human suffering reveals Jesus's power and compassion in such a dramatic way. We shouldn't think rigidly, "God allowed this child to have leukemia so that God could be glorified." Suffering is much more mysterious and tragic than that. But God can and will reveal his power and compassion amid our suffering, and we can invite him to do so.

4. Martha believes Jesus is the Messiah and the Son of God. She believes he has the power to heal the sick. She even believes her brother will be raised from the dead with all faithful Jews at the end of the age (the Pharisees also believed in this resurrection at the end of the age). Does Jesus want her to believe he has such power over not just sickness, but death, that he can raise Lazarus immediately? He does, but it's hard for us to blame her for the limits of her faith—who of us would trust him more than she?

6. The temple (their religion, and for the priests their livelihood) is at stake. Their nation—their political system, in which they have power—is at stake. Power, money, and one's religious assumptions will motivate a great many of us to do terrible things, or to stand by while others do them. They claim to be doing what is good for their faith and their people, but they are unwilling to consider that what is really good for their faith and their people might cost them what they hold dear.

7. At their home, Mary anoints Jesus's feet with expensive perfume; the cost was probably about a year's wages at that time. She is probably profoundly grateful for what Jesus has done for her brother and her family. This is an act of deep and sacrificial love. Also, women in her culture simply don't do things like this toward men—they don't even take down their hair in front of men, let alone wipe their hair on a man's feet. Mary is opening herself to public shame, but she doesn't care.

8. His response shows that he knows he is God (and so deserves the kind of worship that would be utterly wrong for anybody else) and that he knows he will die in less than a week (and so will need Jewish burial rites, which often involve this kind of perfumed ointment to mask the odor of decay).

Jesus is a unique mix of deep humility and unapologetic assertion that he is God and should be treated that way. Anybody else who acted like God as Jesus does could hardly be called humble.

9. Has Jesus done anything for us that deserves our passionate gratitude? Yes. Should we be as unconcerned about what other people think of us as she is? Probably. Do we worship Jesus with that kind of love?
11. Jesus enters Jerusalem in triumph, as a king, but on a donkey, fulfilling Zechariah 9:9. The donkey is the mount of a man of peace, and the context of Zechariah drives home the peacemaking nature of this king. John 12:16 indicates that not even Jesus's disciples are putting the pieces together and discerning what Jesus's actions say about the kind of king he is.
12. Jesus's glory will be revealed paradoxically, through his humiliating death on the cross, and then his resurrection and exaltation. We too need to make the choices of self-sacrifice.

*Developing*

13. This activity provides an opportunity for the group to share Jesus in a very practical way. Discuss this with the group and choose one action step to take as a group. Invite one person to volunteer to be the point person on this. They would investigate the action step you have chosen and report back to the group what they find out next week. For example, if you have chosen to do yard work, then the point person would contact the church to find a needy family and schedule the work to be done. It is ideal that every member of the group participates, but don't wait until all schedules align before making a plan to follow through. Many times, waiting until eight or ten individuals are available can cause a plan to fizzle.
14. If members of the group have committed to spending time alone with God, congratulate them and encourage them to take their commitment one step further and begin journaling. Review *Journaling 101* in the *Appendix* prior to your group meeting so that you are familiar with what it contains.
15. It's time to start thinking about what your group will do when you're finished with this study. Now is the time to ask how many people will be joining you so you can choose a study and have the books available when you meet for the last session.

*Sharing*

16. It is important to return to the *Circles of Life* often, both to encourage the group to follow through on their commitments as well as to foster growth toward new commitments. Encourage the group this week to consider

reaching out to their non-Christian friends, family, and acquaintances. Remind everyone that our responsibility is to share Jesus with others, but it is the Holy Spirit's responsibility to convict souls and bring forth change.

17. Encourage group members to consider developing their salvation story as a tool for sharing their faith with others. Begin the process during your group time and encourage the group to complete the exercise at home. As leader, you should review the "Tips" section of *Telling Your Story* yourself in advance and be ready to share your ideas about this process with the group.

18. Encourage group members to think about when they are shepherding another person in Christ. This could be simply following through on inviting someone to church or reaching out to them in Christ's love. Then have everyone answer the question "WHEN are you shepherding another person in Christ?" on the *Personal Health Plan.*

## Session Seven The Last Supper and the Farewell Discourse

*Growing*

This session covers John 13–17. Since this is a large volume of material, we recommend asking the group to read the selection at home before arriving for study. As you progress through the study, portions of the entire content have been selected for group reading and discussion.

3. Jesus chooses this opportunity to model true humility and what it means to live life in selfless service to others. He will soon model this to the fullest in his death on the cross.

5. At first Peter refuses to let Jesus wash his feet. He is appalled that Jesus would take on a role his society sees as shameful. He doesn't understand that Jesus has turned notions of honor and humiliation on their heads, and has made servanthood the key to greatness.

6. Jesus says that if Peter refuses to let him wash his feet, Peter will have no part with him. His response to Peter looks beyond the refusal to the condition of Peter's heart, which is split between humility and pride. Peter needs spiritual cleansing, and Jesus's washing of Peter's feet symbolizes this cleansing.

8. John doesn't just happen to mention what time it is. Night represents spiritual darkness throughout John's Gospel (recall 3:19–20). Judas has followed Jesus along with the other disciples all this time, yet he is unable to see the truth about him as the others are beginning to do. He has never put his trust in the light of the world. He has preferred to hide his heart in darkness; now he gives himself over to the power of darkness.

9. Sacrificial love is the distinguishing mark of Christ's followers and should be evident in all we say and do. The standard by which we measure our love is Christ. If we are to love as Christ did, then we must be willing to serve as he did. Until now in John's Gospel, Jesus has stressed the importance of faith in him as the way to eternal life. Now he says that sacrificial love for others is the mark of one who has saving faith in Christ.

10. In his farewell discourse, Jesus warns the disciples of dangers to come and promises them the presence of the Holy Spirit to guide and protect them. The Spirit will mediate the presence of the Father and the Son to the disciples. The Spirit will teach, guide, and strengthen them. He is the Spirit of truth. He is like an Advocate in a court of law, presenting a case for truth and defending believers against accusations from the world or the evil one.

11. Encourage the group to talk about how the Holy Spirit is an active part of their daily life as they walk with Christ. Some things they might think of are the inner peace and the still small voice we sense when we need wisdom and guidance. They may also agree that God works through other people to meet very real needs for love, support, strength, and wisdom. The Spirit also works through gifted teachers and everyday believers to teach us what is true and right to do.

12. To abide in Christ is to remain in close fellowship with him. This includes things like believing in him, trusting him as our Savior, spending time with him, spending time thinking about what he says in the Bible, talking to him in prayer, paying attention to him as we go through our day, continuing to believe the truth about him even when circumstances disturb us, and loving other believers. Just as a branch is sustained by the vine, we too bear spiritual fruit only by staying close to him. Galatians 5:22–23 speaks of the fruit of the Spirit: love, joy, peace, patience, kindness, goodness, faithfulness, gentleness, and self-control. From John 4:34–36 we also see fruit described as the joy of seeing eternity impacted as people come to Christ.

13. Review the *Spiritual Gifts Inventory* with the group. Affirm those who have served the group or plugged into a ministry and encourage those who have not that it's never too late. If you have people still struggling with identifying their gifts, encourage them to talk to people who know them well. You might want to share what you've seen in them as well.

## Session Eight Arrest, Trial, Crucifixion, and Resurrection

*Growing*

This session covers John 18–21. Since this is a large volume of material, we recommend asking the group to read the selection at home before arriving for study. As you progress through the study, portions of the entire content have been selected for group reading and discussion.

4. Ironically, the faithful Son of God speaks truthfully while the weak disciple lies. Jesus seems willing to face his fate, a fate he has foreseen, with complete trust in his Father. By contrast, Peter is in shock; he didn't see this threat coming, and his faith is shaken.

   At times we may find ourselves fearing the response of others if they find out we are Christians. Many people today look down on Christians and don't mind saying so. Encourage discussion on ways group members can relate to Peter's failure.

5. His kingdom isn't a political one like Rome's. It is rooted beyond this world. It is a realm of the deepest truth, and Jesus came into this world to testify to this truth. Jesus isn't so otherworldly that his kingship has nothing to do with this world. On the contrary, while it can't be established with an army or a ballot box, it has a great deal to do with what we do in this life.

6. While Pilate may believe he is in control, and the Jewish leaders may think they are driving events here, God is sovereign. The fulfillments of Scripture we see in these passages are: the dividing of Jesus's garments (Ps. 22:18), his thirst on the cross and his sipping wine vinegar (Ps. 69:21), his unbroken bones (Exod. 12:46 and Ps. 34:20), the piercing of his side (Zech. 12:10). Jesus makes the situation clear to Pilate in their verbal exchange in John 19:10–11.

7. "It is finished" (19:30) can mean, "Paid in full." Jesus's words mean that salvation for humanity has been accomplished. In the end, Jesus released his spirit. No one is responsible for taking his life; he willingly gives it up. (See John 10:11, 15, 17–18; 15:13 for more insight.)

8. The empty tomb, the angels, and Jesus's conversation with Mary confirm Jesus's resurrection. The strips of linen are lying in the tomb in an orderly fashion. Grave robbers wouldn't bother to unwrap a body, or if they did, they would leave the wrappings scattered.

   Also, Jesus's tender interaction with Mary is noteworthy. As emotional as she understandably is, and as much as she wants to cling to him, their relationship will never be the same, because he has to return to the Father and send the Holy Spirit instead.

9. Jesus has been promising to send the Holy Spirit throughout John's Gospel (4:15; 7:37–39; 14:15; etc), so John includes a glimpse of what that means. Just as Jesus was sent into the world to save the world, not to condemn it (knowing that the world may condemn itself, 3:16–18), so Jesus's followers are sent to offer forgiveness of sins, knowing that those who refuse the offer are choosing judgment. The Holy Spirit within Jesus's followers will convict the world of sin, righteousness, and judgment (16:7–11).

10. This is a chance to summarize what you've learned. Are Jesus's miraculous works convincing? His words? The way he handled himself during his interrogation? The fulfillment of Scripture at his crucifixion? The evidence of his resurrection? Why should someone bet their life that Jesus is who he claims to be in John's Gospel?

*Sharing*

14. Allow one or two group members to share for a few minutes a testimony about how they helped someone connect in Christian community or shared Jesus with an unbelieving friend or relative.

# DEEPENING LIFE TOGETHER SERIES

## New Studies Available!

FRUIT OF THE SPIRIT

JAMES

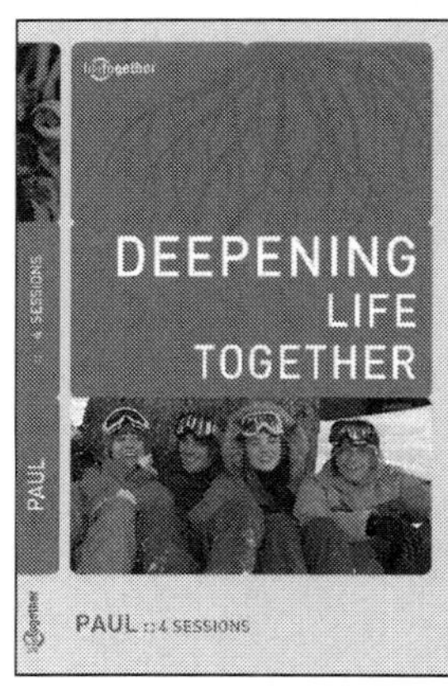


PAUL

PSALMS

RUTH

SERMON ON THE MOUNT

Made in the USA
Middletown, DE
24 February 2020

85255507R20082